Cross Of Death, Tree Of Life

A Sacred Reading of the Story of Redemption

Jerome Machar, O.C.S.O.

AVE MARIA PRESS   Notre Dame, Indiana 46556

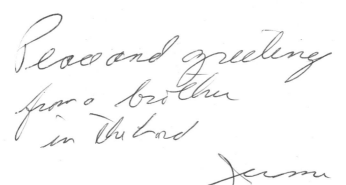

Peace and greeting
from a brother
in the Lord

Jerome

International Standard Book Number: 0-87793-595-5.

0-87793-596-3 (CB)

Cover and interior art by Sr. Ann Therese Kelly, C.S.S.F. Copyright © 1996, all rights reserved.

Cover and text design by Katherine Robinson Coleman.

Printed and bound in the United States of America.

Library of Congress Cataloging-in-Publication Data
Machar, Jerome.
      Cross of death, tree of life : a sacred reading of the story of
  Redemption / Jerome Machar.
          p.   cm.
    Includes bibliographical references.
    ISBN 0-87793-595-5 (paper). — ISBN 0-87793-596-3 (cloth)
    1. Jesus Christ—Biography—Passion Week. 2. Paschal triduum.
    I. Title.
    BT431.M32   1996
    232.96—dc20
                                       96-31297
                                         CIP

"O death, where is your sting?
O Hades, where is your victory?"
Christ is risen and you are abolished . . .
Christ is risen, and life is freed.

Resurrection Homily of St. John Chrysostom

To my parents
Genevieve and Louis Machar
whose love and faith
taught me how to live
for the love of God

Contents

Introduction

Jesus of Nazareth
The Son of God and Son of Man

> Here is a saying that you can rely on and nobody should doubt: that Jesus Christ came into the world to save sinners. I myself am the greatest of them; and if mercy has been shown me, it is because Jesus Christ meant to make me the greatest evidence of his inexhaustible patience for all the other people who would later have to trust in him to come to eternal life (1 Tim 1:15-16).

Among my earliest religious memories is going to church to make the Stations of the Cross. That devotion allowed me to walk with Jesus the path of love and mercy which brought about universal salvation and redemption. One line from the booklets used in those days went something like this, "I love you, Jesus, my love; grant that I might love you always and then do with me what you will." The passion of our Lord and Savior Jesus Christ is the story of God's undying love for each and every member of the human family. Having felt this love, I offer this collection of my reflections because the story needs to be told again and again in various ways until the message resounds in the heart of each and every individual.

The four canonical gospels narrate the passion, death, and resurrection of Jesus, each presenting a slightly different aspect of the events. Spiritual writers have retold the same story, stressing either the human desolation and pain of the

Lord, or his abiding glory as the eternal Son of God. Indeed, there seems to be no lack of interest in the events which went to make up the last week of Jesus' life. Scholars continue to offer insights, and these pages will not settle the debates. What I offer here are the reflections and insights which I have received after years of prayerful *lectio divina*.

Lectio divina—"sacred reading"—is an ancient practice of reading the word of God, repeating the words aloud until they are committed to memory and pondered in the heart. This reverent recital of the word often creates a resonance with other words which have been gathered from other sources, be they religious or secular. The harmony and mingling of the sounds, both old and new, draw our personal life experience into the mystery of God's ever unfolding plan of salvation. *Lectio divina* allows us to carry the word of God with us while we fulfill our daily tasks. The repetition of the word allows all of the created reality to resound with the message of life.

We find Jesus himself employing *lectio divina*. When he initiated his ministry in the synagogue in Nazareth, Jesus declared that he understood his mission in terms of the prophet Isaiah. He knew the text of the prophet; he had heard it read and interpreted by the scholars of his day. Starting with their teaching, he expanded upon it by reading his own life into the text. These insights would be clarified by hours of prayerful communion with the Father. When Jesus met with his disciples after he had been raised from the dead, he likewise spoke to them of the Law and the Prophets as they applied to the Messiah.

As we practice *lectio divina*, we make Jesus' method of interpreting the sacred texts our own. And so, while I touch on current exegetical, archaeological, and historical research, it is primarily *lectio divina* which informs this book. I hope the reading of these pages will help you to know better the love of him who came down to earth so that we might be raised up to heaven.

The life of Jesus has been presented in many forms: movies and stage productions, magazine articles and books, lectures and debates. Each presentation has had its own bias; e.g. the tragic death of a beloved teacher, the foreknowledge of resurrection glory, the rejection of its glory by Israel, the vindication of the gospel. Some depict the crucifixion as the glorious martyrdom of a revolutionary leader. Some have even used the passion story as an excuse for anti-Semitism and violence. To hold to any one of these views, however, would cause one to depart from the biblical and faith tradition of Israel and of the early church.

The gospels tell us that Jesus did, in fact, die on the cross. He was betrayed by one of the members of his inner circle. Having been tried before the Jewish leaders, his name was removed from the Book of the Living, and he was no longer numbered among the People of God. He was handed over to the court of Rome and executed as a common criminal, only to be acknowledged as the "Son of God" in his death. All this we learn from the text; it is what has often been called the literal sense. To restrict ourselves to the information provided by the literal sense, however, would quickly render the actual events sterile and lifeless. The Holy Spirit, who inspired the writings, dwells within them and grants a spiritual understanding to any who would read them.

In addition to the literal sense, patristic and monastic writers specify three spiritual senses of scripture: the allegorical sense, the moral sense, and the anagogical sense. The lines dividing them are not always distinct, but they can be summarized as follows: the allegorical sense allows us to interpret the scriptural events in light of their relationship to Christ; the moral sense helps us to see how the text governs our behavior; and the anagogical sense allows us to view the text in terms of our final goal, anticipating our eternal homeland in heaven. Closely connected to reading scripture for its spiritual sense is the belief that, thanks to the unity of God's salvific plan, texts from one book of scripture can be used to gain insight into events of another. In preparing this project, I have aligned myself with the fathers of the church and with the ancient monastic writers in attempting to uncover the spiritual sense of the passion narratives. I will here read the Books of Moses, the Law, and the Prophets, as windows to understanding the

Passover of Jesus of Nazareth, the Christ of God.

For people living in a highly technical society, the tendency is toward the clarity and distinctions found in the literal sense, as presented by modern exegesis. While spiritual levels of interpretation lack the same precision, they tend to allow a more holistic approach to the message of God's loving kindness. This approach goes beyond the head and speaks to the heart, both of the text and of the reader. We can thereby encounter Jesus, the only Son of God, who became Son of Israel, and who related to his Father in terms of the faith of Israel. This living and life-giving exchange can enrich our understanding of the Christian faith in light of a more ancient experience of the one true God.

The insights one receives through *lectio divina* and through attention to scripture's spiritual senses do not always follow a precise or clear path of development. I will be the first to admit that there are obvious weaves, swerves, and reverses throughout this text. The sight of such an untidy terrain will frighten some and tempt them to head for the comfort of the literal sense, provided by scientific exegesis. To them I say: don't be afraid! For a moment, set your literal bias aside and try reading the scriptures with your heart. Such an approach may open a new world of possibilities for you.

I began this introduction with a quote from 1 Timothy. Paul saw his life as integrally related to God's eternal plan of salvation, and so should we. Our status as "sinners," being members of a "fallen race" dates back to Adam and Eve. Along with the fall, however, came the promise of salvation: standing beneath the tree of temptation, God foretold the victorious struggle between the "son of the woman" and the serpent. Through the passion narratives we stand beneath the tree of life, where this promise is fulfilled. The first chapter of this project, therefore, is devoted to establishing Jesus as the Son of the Woman, building on the traditional understanding of Mary as the New Eve. While this is not a part of the passion story, *per se*, it is important for us to see Jesus as one who was nurtured in the faith of Israel. This idea of beginning the passion story with Mary is not original. It was borrowed from the

Passion Play of Oberammergau, Germany, in which Jesus bids Mary an emotional farewell before he enters Jerusalem.

As you read along, don't be too surprised by the material you will encounter; much of it fell into place through a process of free association. Those who are old enough to remember the game charades will recall the phrase, "sounds like. . . ." So, too, here: a line in the passion story "sounded like" something I had read or seen, and so it was noted in the text. As you read along, you may have similar moments of recall which help you appreciate the wonders of God's love. Actually, that is the joy of *lectio*. May the Lord who inspired this work bring it to completion in the Day of Christ Jesus.

                    Jerome Machar, O.C.S.O.
                    Abbey of Genesee

One

In the Beginning . . .

Before beginning our reflections on the passion events, it is necessary to pause and examine the notion that salvation is a part of God's divine plan from the beginning of human existence. St. John gives us a glimpse of this truth when he relates the conversation which took place between Jesus and Nicodemus. "Yes, God loved the world so much that he gave his only Son, so that everyone who believes in him may not be lost but may have eternal life. For God sent his Son into the world not to condemn the world, but so that through him the world might be saved" (Jn. 3:16-17).

The attitude of God towards all of creation is one of love. "God saw all he had made, and indeed it was very good. Evening came and morning came: the sixth day" (Gn. 1:31). Jesus told Nicodemus that what the Father saw as good, he loved. And the goodness that God saw and loved was not lost, even though it was contaminated by original sin. Thus the Son comes not to condemn, but to redeem our sinful race by re-establishing our lost innocence. In the Word-Made-Flesh, God again sees the primal goodness, the perfect reflection of his image and likeness.

In Christ, not only would the curse brought upon the whole of creation through Adam's infidelity be removed, but a blessing would be imparted. Now would come the reversal of the curse spoken in the garden. "Because you listened to the voice of your wife and ate from the tree of which I had forbidden you to eat, accursed be the soil because of you. With suffering shall

11

you get food from it every day of your life. It shall yield you brambles and thistles, and you shall eat wild plants. With sweat on your brow shall you eat your bread, until you return to the soil, as you were taken from it. For dust you are and to dust you shall return" (Gn. 3:17-19).

St. Paul also stresses this concept of purgation and restoration in the letter to the Romans.

> Adam prefigured the One to come, but the gift itself considerably outweighed the fall. If it is certain that through one man's fall so many died, it is even more certain that divine grace, coming through the one man Jesus Christ, came to so many as an abundant free gift. The results of the gift also outweigh the results of one man's sin: for after one single fall came judgment with a verdict of condemnation, now after many falls comes grace with its verdict of acquittal. If it is certain that death reigned over everyone as the consequence of one man's fall, it is even more certain that one man, Jesus Christ, will cause everyone to reign in life who receives the free gift that he does not deserve, of being made righteous (Rom. 5:15-17).

Very often spiritual writers speak of God's plan for salvation in terms of justice or restitution. Yet Jesus identified the coming of the Son of Man as the direct result of God's fidelity to his people in loving kindness. Thus Paul can refer to redemption as "an abundant free gift." The notion of God's loving kindness is taken up in the Johanine writings, as well: "God's love for us was revealed when God sent into the world his only Son so that we could have life through him; this is the love I mean: not our love for God, but God's love for us when he sent his Son to be the sacrifice that takes our sins away" (1 Jn. 4:9-10).

God's love was manifested to us in the Son, who emptied himself of all the glory that was his as God and laid down his life on our behalf. In order to understand more deeply the idea that Jesus' passion and death did not merely fulfill the just punishment levied as a result of original sin, it is necessary to keep in mind an interpretation of the word "sacrifice" which speaks of more than making restitution. To sacrifice can also mean to risk the loss of one's own life or the life of a loved one so that others may live; we see this, for example, in David's sacrificial choice to fight Goliath as Israel's champion.

Closely related to this broader definition of sacrifice is the notion of *goel* or "avenger," as found in the Hebrew scriptures. Try reading the following section of Genesis while keeping the idea of champion or avenger in mind: "Then Yahweh God said to the Serpent, 'Because you have done this, be accursed beyond all cattle, all wild beasts. You shall crawl on your belly and eat dust every day of your life. I will make you enemies of each other: you and the woman, your offspring and her offspring. It will crush your head and you will strike its heel'"(Gn. 3:14-15).

God so loved the world that his only Son became the son of the woman. As the son of the woman, he would enter into mortal combat with the infernal Serpent. Let there be no misunderstanding about it: like the combat between David and Goliath, this would be a fight to the death. In the end, the conqueror would despoil the vanquished of all his booty. This is clearly stated in the oration David delivered before engaging with Goliath.

> You come against me with sword and spear and javelin, but I come against you in the name of Yahweh Sabaoth, the God of Armies, the armies of Israel, that you have dared to insult. Today Yahweh will deliver you into my hands and I shall kill you; I will cut off your head, and this very day I will give your dead body and the bodies of the Philistine army to the birds of the air and the wild beasts of the earth, so that all the earth may know that there is a God in Israel, and that all this assembly may know that it is not by sword or by spear that Yahweh gives the victory, for Yahweh is Lord of the battle and he will deliver you into our power (1 Sam. 17:45-47).

In the battle which Jesus takes up, the opponent is not Rome, nor is it Israel; he does not enter into contest with the Pharisees or the Sadducees; neither does he contend against

Judas nor the rabble in the streets. The struggle is much more primal; it is the battle between the Prince of Darkness and the Prince of Light. Jesus stands before Pilate as the champion or avenger *(goel)* of the entire human race. Hanging in the balance is the eternal fate of every man, woman, and child ever to walk to face of the earth. "Now sentence is being passed on this world; now the prince of this world is to be overthrown. And when I am lifted up from the earth, I shall draw all men to myself" (Jn. 12:31-32). "For the Son of Man must be lifted up as Moses lifted up the serpent in the desert, so that everyone who believes may have eternal life in him" (Jn. 3:13-15).

It is important that we do not read these familiar passages of scriptures too hastily. To do so might cause us to miss the subtle way in which Jesus transforms the image of "being lifted up." The passage to which Jesus alludes comes from Numbers: "Yahweh answered Moses, 'Make a fiery serpent and put it on a standard. If anyone is bitten and looks at it, he shall live.' So Moses fashioned a bronze serpent which he put on a standard, and if anyone was bitten by a serpent, he looked at the bronze serpent and lived" (Num. 21:8-9). Jesus is the Son of the Woman whose heel was bitten by the snake, but he is also the one who crushed the head of the snake once and for all. Jesus is lifted up as victorious conqueror and not as conquered victim. No longer are we to look upon the fiery serpent; from this day forward, we are to look upon him who crushed the head of the serpent and behold him who is the Lord of Life. "They will look upon the one whom they have pierced" (Jn. 19:37). Oh, that we might see the glory of him who was pierced for our sake and that we might share in his glory for all eternity.

Should you scan the scriptures, you would find further insights into the Son of the Woman who would engage the infernal serpent in mortal combat. To vanquish the Prince of Darkness he would enter into Sheol, the land of shadows. To conquer death he would die and thus crush the head of the Prince of Death. "The Lord himself, therefore, will give you a sign. It is this: the maiden is with child and will soon give birth to a son whom she will call Immanuel [God is with us]" (Is.

7:14). Even after the first members of the human family sinned and fell from original innocence, God did not desert the creatures he had made for himself. God did not abandon humanity to its fate, but rather, promised to send a *goel* who would contend with the serpent and, in the contest, prove that God was with his people. The mysterious maiden mentioned in Isaiah is identified for us by Luke. "And the virgin's name was Mary" (Lk. 1:27). Mary is the new Eve. It is her son who will fulfill the promise made by God as Adam and Eve were banished from the garden.

In order to have a clear understanding of redemption, we need to be familiar with its foreshadowing in the Old Testament. The first woman stood beneath the branches of the tree knowing that the fruit of her womb would inherit turmoil and death; the second woman stands beneath the arms of the cross knowing that the fruit of her womb would bring all people to peace and the fullness of life. The first was seduced by the serpent; the second placed herself at the service of God and gave birth to the one who would crush the serpent's head.

"Adam and Eve heard the sound of God walking in the garden in the cool of the day, and they hid from God among the trees of the garden" (Gn. 3:8). Having fallen from innocence, Adam and Eve were filled with shame at the presence of God who had been their friend. Having been sustained in her innocence, Mary delights in God's presence. Although she is troubled by the nature of the angel's greeting, she does not run, neither does she hide from him. "Mary, do not be afraid; you have won God's favor" (Lk. 1:30).

This joyful, obedient response to the "sound of God walking" is elsewhere extolled. "Eli said to Samuel, 'Go and lie down, and if someone calls, say: Speak, Yahweh, your servant is listening'" (1 Sam. 3:9). Samuel learns to listen to—which, in Hebrew also means to "obey"—the life-giving voice of God. It was at a word of Yahweh that the world came into being; likewise, it was at a word of Yahweh that the world came to redemption and recreation. The word of God is a life-giving gift, and only by remaining in his presence does one come to know the fullness of grace which he brings.

The word spoken by the Serpent, on the other hand, brought sin and death into the world. "The woman saw that the tree was good to eat and pleasing to the eye, and that it was desirable for the knowledge it could give. So she took some of its fruit and ate it. She gave some also to her husband who was with her, and he ate it. Then the eyes of both of them were opened and they realized that they were naked" (Gn. 3:6-7).

The angel of light, on the other hand, spoke a word of promise to the virgin of Nazareth. "You are to conceive and bear a son, and you must name him Jesus. He will be great and will be called Son of the Most High. The Lord God will give him the throne of his ancestor David; he will rule over the House of Jacob for ever and his reign will have no end" (Lk. 1:31-33). Unlike her predecessor, the second Eve knew neither desire nor shame, only humble submission to the will of God whose servant she knew herself to be.

The moment of truth for the second Eve was different from that of the first. Following the example of her husband, the first Eve did not take responsibility for her misdeed. Pointing an accusing finger, she neither confessed her guilt nor sought mercy and forgiveness. "The serpent tempted me and I ate" (Gn. 3:13). Like her sinful children after her, she attempted to blame God for her fall from innocence; had God not created the serpent nor created the delightful tree, she never would have sinned. This complaint is amplified in the letter to the Romans. "Once, when there was no law, I was alive; but when the commandment came, sin came to life and I died: the commandment was meant to lead me to life, but it turned out to mean death for me, because sin took advantage of the commandment to mislead me, and so sin, through that commandment, killed me" (Rom. 7:9-11). Both Adam and Eve covered their shame with pride and refused to bow down in reverence to the Holy One who created them. In sharp contrast is Mary, the second Eve, who hears the word of God which is addressed to her and places herself at the service of the Holy One who has called her name. "I am the handmaid of the Lord, let what you have said be done to me" (Lk. 1:38).

How rightly is it said: the refusal to thus submit to God

leads only to ruin. When people lust after what is not rightfully theirs, not only do they not attain what they desire, but they
also lose that which is properly theirs. Consequently, they
spend more and more time, exerting more and more energy, to
get that which they don't even truly want. "So God expelled
Adam from the garden of Eden, to till the soil from which he
had been taken. He banished the man, and in front of the garden of Eden he posted the cherubs, and the flame of a flashing
sword, to guard the way to the tree of life" (Gn. 3:23-24). Adam
and Eve were escorted out of the garden. No longer were they
to enjoy the afternoon strolls with the God who created them.
To frustrate any attempt to return, an angel was posted at the
gate. Significantly, after Mary made her act of submission, "the
angel left her" (Lk. 1:38). At that moment, it is God who over-
shadows her with his presence and the only-begotten Son
makes his dwelling within her virginal womb. The time of
redemption and reconciliation had come.

We find the announcement of the time of redemption in the
Book of Revelation, as well. Multiple interpretations are given
for the image of the "woman" depicted there. Some suggest
that she signifies Israel as the mother of the messianic age; others suggest that she signifies the church as the mother of the
body of Christ; still others suggest that the woman signifies
Mary, the Mother of God. In this book, I will take up the interpretation of the woman as Mary, the Mother of God.

"Now . . . a great sign appeared in heaven: a woman,
adorned with the sun, standing on the moon, and with the
twelve stars on her head for a crown. She was pregnant, and
in labor, crying aloud in the pangs of childbirth" (Rv. 12:1-2).
At the end of the annunciation narrative, the angel of light
departs. Mary conceives a son and within her chaste womb the
Son of God finds a suitable abode. "This is how Jesus Christ
came to be born. His mother Mary was betrothed to Joseph;
but before they came to live together she was found to be with
child through the Holy Spirit (Mt. 1:18). Mary becomes the
portal, the gateway to the eternal kingdom, through whom the
King of Kings and the Master of the Universe will again come
into his garden and walk among his creatures.

"Then a second sign appeared in the sky, a huge red dragon which had seven heads and ten horns, and each of the
seven heads was crowned with a coronet. Its tail dragged a
third of the stars from the sky and dropped them to the earth"
(Rv. 12:3-4a). The incarnation, the encounter between the Son
of God and the Serpent, has cosmic effects. The heavens themselves give testimony to the presence of God and the expression of his loving kindness, his desire to avenge the wrong
done to his children, Adam and Eve. "Some wise men came to
Jerusalem from the East. 'Where is the infant king of the Jews?'
they asked. 'We saw his star as it rose and have come to do him
homage'" (Mt. 2:1b-2).

No sooner than the child is brought into this world does the
conflict with the Serpent begin. "The dragon stopped in front
of the woman as she was having the child, so that he could eat
it as soon as it was born from its mother" (Rv. 12:4b). As in the
garden, the Serpent uses human instruments in an effort to
frustrate the design of the Holy One. When the plot fails, Satan
makes a direct attack. "Herod was furious when he realized
that he had been outwitted by the wise men, and in Bethlehem
and its surrounding district he had all the male children killed
who were two years old or under, reckoning by the date he
had been careful to ask the wise men" (Mt. 1:16). "So the serpent vomited water from his mouth, like a river, after the
woman to sweep her away in the current, but the earth came
to her rescue, it opened its mouth and swallowed the river
thrown up by the dragon's jaws" (Rv. 12:15-16). The murderous rage of Herod, the condemnation and blasphemy of
Caiaphas, and the spewing mouth of the serpent are images
depicting the fulfillment of the promise made by God in the
garden (cf. Gn. 3:14-15).

In the account of the slaughter of the innocent children of
Bethlehem is heard the echo of killing of the Hebrew children
ordered by Pharaoh in Egypt. "Pharaoh then gave his subjects
this command: 'Throw all the boys born to the Hebrews into the
river, but let all the girls live'" (Ex. 1:22). The God of Israel, who
heard the mournful cries of his people in Egypt, is the Father of
the Word-Made-Flesh, who heard the sobs of his people in

Bethlehem. As promised of old, he would be their *goel.*

"The woman escaped into the desert, where God had made a place of safety ready" (Rv. 12:6). "The angel of the Lord appeared to Joseph in a dream and said, 'Get up, take the child and his mother with you, and escape into Egypt'" (Mt. 2:13). God is our redeemer, our savior, and his purpose will prevail. "I am your brother Joseph whom you sold into Egypt. But now, do not grieve, do not reproach yourselves for having sold me here, since God sent me before you to preserve your lives" (Gn. 45:5).

"After Herod's death, the angel of the Lord appeared in a dream to Joseph in Egypt and said, 'Get up, take the child and his mother with you and go back to the land of Israel, for those who wanted to kill the child are dead.' So Joseph got up and, taking the child and mother with him, went back to the land of Israel" (Mt. 2:19-21). The lived experience of Israel becomes the lived experience of the "woman and her offspring." The assaults of the Evil One bring about a period of exile from the land of promise. With the Passover of the Lord, however, the bonds of slavery are broken and the period of exile is ended; the children of the promise are brought home and reclaim their heritage.

This restoration includes also reconciliation with God. Solomon had prayed for this reconciliation when he prayed to God for his people:

> If they sin against you—for there is no man who does not sin—and you are angry with them and deliver them to the enemy, and their conquerors lead them captive to a country far or near, if in the land of the exile they come to themselves and repent, and in the country of their conquerors they entreat you saying, "We have sinned, we have acted perversely and wickedly," and if they turn again to you with all their heart and soul in the country of the enemies who have deported them, and pray to you, turning towards the land you gave to our ancestors, towards the city you have chosen, and towards the Temple I have built for your name, hear from heaven where your home is, forgive your people the sins they have committed against you and all the

> crimes they have been guilty of, grant them to win
> favour with their conquerors so that they may have
> pity on them; for they are your people and your her-
> itage whom you brought out of Egypt, that iron furnace
> (1 Kgs. 8:46-51).

If a sinner makes a confession of guilt and turns toward the
Holy Place, let that one find a hearing and forgiveness. This
very message was contained in the comment made by Jesus to
Nicodemus. If the sinner turns to the Holy One who has been
lifted up on the tree, that one will find eternal life. The
dwelling place of God is on earth because he has chosen to
dwell among his people; not only that, he has chosen to
become one of them. Through the incarnation, he has united
human nature to his divine nature, and this bond can never be
severed or broken.

By faithfully living out her commitment to the God of Israel
and by coming to the Temple in Jerusalem, Mary learns more
about this, the true identity of her son. The new dwelling place
of the Lord, upon whose virginal breasts the God of the
Universe finds a throne, comes to the Temple made by human
hands. "Simeon blessed them and said to Mary his mother,
'You see this child: he is destined for the fall and for the rising
of many in Israel, destined to be a sign that is rejected so that
the secret thoughts of many may be laid bare. And a sword
will pierce your own soul too'" (Lk. 2:34-35).

The woman who appeared robed in the sun will see her son
wrapped in darkness. As she sees her only son lifted up on the
cross, she will feel the pain of the sword nearly cutting her in
two. Only then, when the sun seems to be eclipsed, will the
glory of God's justice be made manifest. "On these grounds is
sentence pronounced: that though the light has come into the
world men have shown they prefer darkness to the light
because their deeds were evil. And indeed, everybody who
does wrong hates the light and avoids it, for fear his actions
should be exposed but the man who lives by the truth comes
out into the light, so that it may be plainly seen that what he
does is done in God" (Jn. 3:20-21). The struggle between Jesus
and Satan now becomes the moment of truth for all the members

of the human family. Are their hearts filled with light or darkness? Are they children of the night or children of the day?

Children of the day, like the mother of the light, will leave
everything once they realize the absence of the light and then
go and seek him. We can enter into Mary's pain and longing as
we read the account of Jesus' being found in the Temple.
"They were overcome when they saw him, and his mother
said to him, 'My child, why have you done this to us? See how
worried your father and I have been, looking for you'" (Lk.
2:48). The concern of the mother is not unlike the yearning of
the bride for her beloved. "I sought him whom my heart loves.
I sought but did not find him. So I will rise and go through the
city; in the streets and the squares I will seek him whom my
heart loves" (Sg. 3:1-2). Recognizing the void in our life, we
cannot remain in it. It is as if God were pulling us out of the
darkness and drawing us toward the light. "Then I found him
whom my heart loves, I held him fast, nor would I let him go
until I had brought him into my mother's house, into the room
of her who conceived me" (Sg. 3:4). Jesus is the beloved; he is
the only-begotten Son who has become the object of Mary's
search. He is the only one able to fill the void in her, and our,
life. "He then went down with them and came to Nazareth
and lived under their authority. His mother stored up all these
things in her heart" (Lk. 2:51). Having found the beloved,
there is peace and the fullness of joy. All that is darkness and
sin has been driven away. "Wine flowing straight to my
Beloved, as it runs on the lips of those who sleep. I am my
beloved's, and his desire is for me" (Sg. 7:10-11).

Life in Nazareth and the relationships which existed
among Jesus, Mary, and Joseph can only be conjectured. No
one can tell how long Mary and Joseph were married before
Joseph died. Neither can we be certain how old Jesus was
when he actually left the family hearth to begin his public ministry. "Now as the time drew near for him to be taken up to
heaven, Jesus resolutely took the road for Jerusalem" (Lk.
9:51). Jerusalem was the city of the great King David; the place
where Solomon had built the Temple which became the center
of worship for the people of Israel. No doubt, the thought of

her son going to Jerusalem must have filled Mary's heart with fear. Did not the orders to kill the innocent children of Bethlehem come from that city? Did not the priest Simeon tell her of his rejection and her own heartache in Jerusalem? When Jesus was twelve, did she not once lose him in that city? Had not Herod recently arrested and beheaded John, the son of her cousin Elizabeth?

The scriptures do not give us any account of the actual parting. We can only surmise what may have been said between the mother and son as they bade farewell. A certain tension must have filled the air; both were very much aware that Jesus' hour had finally come. It was time for him to leave his mother's home and return to his Father's house. It was time for him to leave his mother's loving embrace and be surrendered into the hands of cruel and vicious men. "There he would be rejected by the elders and the chief priests and the scribes" (Mk. 8:31). "They will condemn him to death and will hand him over to the pagans" (Mk. 10:33). "He will be mocked, maltreated and spat on, and when they have scourged him they will put him to death; and on the third day he will rise again" (Lk. 18:32-33).

In dealing with the topic of the relationship between mother and son, it is essential that we avoid two extremes: depicting a scene which is melodramatic and saccharine and developing a characterization of either mother or son as stoic and dispassionate. Luke repeatedly mentions that Mary pondered the events of her son's life. Certainly she would have tried to balance the words of Gabriel against the murderous attempt on the life of her newborn infant. She could not have forgotten the nightly visits of the peasant sheep herders nor the homage rendered by the oriental dignitaries. Certainly the words of Simeon would be recalled as Jesus spoke of his impending death. It is reasonable to surmise that the mother who questioned her son at the age of twelve would question him now: "But how could your death serve any purpose?"

Searching through the scriptures, we can find hints of an answer in the Gospel of John. "I know that you are descended from Abraham; but in spite of that you want to kill me because nothing I say has penetrated into you. What I, for my part, speak of is what I have seen with my Father; but you, you put into action the lessons learnt from your father" (Jn. 8:37-38). "As it is, you want to kill me when I tell you the truth as I have learnt it from God; and that is not what Abraham did. What you are doing is what your father does" (Jn. 8:40). "The devil is your father, and you prefer to do what your father wants. He was a murderer from the start; he was never grounded in the Truth; there is no truth in him at all: when he lies he is drawing on his own store, because he is a liar, and the father of lies" (Jn. 8:44). "A child of God listens to the words of God; if you refuse to listen, it is because you are not God's children" (Jn. 8:47). "Now sentence is being passed on this world; now the prince of this world is to be overthrown. And when I am lifted up from the earth, I shall draw all men to myself" (Jn. 12:31-32).

At long last, the Woman has brought forth her child, given birth to a son, the one who was to contend with the infernal Serpent. Now the light of truth would shine, and the darkness would be seen for what it was. "All that came to be had life in him and that life was the light of men, a light that shines in the dark, a light that darkness could not overpower" (Jn. 1:4-5).

Trying to understand what Jesus was saying, Mary might have recalled the conversation she once had with the angel Gabriel. None of this really made sense, yet neither did the idea of giving birth to a child without the involvement of a man. How many times had she pondered the words: "Nothing is impossible to God" (Lk. 1:37)? As mother and son faced each other for the last time before he set out to meet his fate, the words she heard coming from his lips must have torn at her heart, even though she knew that God's plans were much greater than anything human beings could ever devise. Ever since the day that she chose unconditional submission, she had to watch with wonder as the events of her life unfolded. Granted, there had been moments of anxiety, fear and sorrow, but never did she revoke her act of self-surrender. Even now, as her son bade farewell and his words drove the sword deeper into her heart, all she could say was, "Let it be done as the Father wills."

Then with an embrace, an exchange of glances, they part. The "hour" has come and the fulfillment of the eternal promise is now at hand. One can only wonder: did Mary understand the meaning of the reference to the resurrection on the third day? Did the emotion of the moment deafen her to the message of hope? We will never know for certain until we meet in that heavenly homeland.

Between mother and son was a certainty that they would be together again before the ordeal ended. Their sentiments can best be found in the Song of Songs. "Set me like a seal on your heart, like a seal on your arm. For love is strong as Death, jealousy relentless as Sheol. The flash of it is a flash of fire, a flame of Yahweh himself. Love no flood can quench, no torrents drown" (Sg. 8:6-7).

Two

Pilgrimage of Freedom

The Passover Feast: The Day Israel Was Set Free from Bondage

The pilgrimage to Jerusalem to celebrate the Feast of Passover was one of the three ritual journeys mandated by the Law of Moses.

> Three times a year you are to celebrate a feast in my honor. You must celebrate the feast of Unleavened Bread: you must eat unleavened bread, as I have commanded you, at the appointed time in the month of Abib, for in that month you came out of the land of Egypt. And no one must come before me empty-handed. The feast of the Harvest, too, you must celebrate, the feast of the first-fruits of the produce of your sown fields; the feast of Ingathering also, at the end of the year when you gather in the fruit of your labors from the fields. Three times a year all your menfolk must present themselves before the Lord Yahweh (Ex. 23:14-17).

As one of the "pilgrim" feasts, the Passover held a special place in the lives of all Jews. Observant Jews would make great sacrifices to make the journey to the Holy City, Jerusalem. Jesus was the child of observant Jews, and so the pilgrimage to Jerusalem would have been a part of his upbringing. This is attested to in the Gospel of Luke. "Every year his parents used to go to Jerusalem for the feast of Passover. When he was twelve years old, they went up for the feast as usual" (Lk. 2:41-42). Palm Sunday, therefore, would not have been the only time Jesus had entered the Temple precincts at the Passover time.

Psalms 120 through 134 have been dubbed the "Hymns of Ascent"; these hymns were sung during the feasts of pilgrimage. "How I rejoiced when they said to me, 'Let us go to the house of Yahweh!' And now our feet are standing in your gateways, Jerusalem" (Ps. 122:1-2). The city of Jerusalem was the center of Jewish cult and history. Besides the Temple, there were monuments which were erected to the memory of David and Solomon. During the annual pilgrimage, old acquaintances could be renewed, the stories of past pilgrimages could be handed on from one generation to the next, and historical events could be brought to life as significant locations or memorial stones were pointed out and identified. By making the trek, the observant Jew could leave behind his urbane concerns and redirect his attention toward God, the Maker of the Universe. By leaving the homestead and social structures which had developed around it, one could intensify attachment to the covenant which God had established with his chosen people through his promise to Abraham. The sacred return to the holy city allowed the pilgrims a carefully structured entry into a world where the ideal of the covenant could be felt, at least for a moment. Even the less observant could find the path to renewed fervor. As the city walls came into sight, one can only imagine the emotions which the tired and excited pilgrims may have felt.

The apostles, though, must have had mixed feelings as they entered the city with their Master. There had been growing animosity toward Jesus, and the crowd of devotees had been dwindling in size. Recently, Jesus' teaching had become more challenging and harder to understand. Charismatic preachers and miracle workers can spark enthusiasm for a while; but the sparkle and thrill quickly fade and with it the interest of the crowds. With the waning of admiration comes the growth of cynicism. Cynicism gives way to contempt which, in turn, eventually turns to hatred. The apostles had seen the crowds; they had heard the arguments with the scribes and Pharisees; they reportedly objected to the wisdom of Jesus' going up to Jerusalem at this time. Emotions would be peaked and it would not take much to inflame the crowd against him, a situation which could prove fatal. But Jesus was driven by a sense of urgency: he had a vision of the coming of the kingdom and he knew that he was somehow to be instrumental in bringing it about. To all the loving concern of the apostles and their attempts to counsel him otherwise, we can only imagine Jesus replying in words similar to those addressed to Mary when he was age twelve. "Did you not know that I must be busy with my Father's affairs?" (Lk. 2:49).

Scanning the gospels one finds indications that the whole of Jesus' life was guided and directed by his perception of the Father's will. Whether the reaction of the crowd was favorable or not, he continued to do and say that which he was convinced the Father wanted done or said. Not only was Jesus a mystic or visionary, he was also an observant Jew, fulfilling the traditional requirements of the Law. It would be inconceivable for him to avoid making the pilgrimage. Fidelity to the covenant was more important than avoiding potential danger. To demur in acting on his vision would be the equivalent of being unfaithful. We are reminded of the death speech of Eleazar. "Even though for the moment I avoid execution by man, I can never, living or dead, elude the grasp of the Almighty. Therefore, if I am man enough to quit this life here and now I shall prove myself worthy of my old age, and I shall have left the young a noble example of how to make a good death, eagerly and generously, for the venerable and holy laws" (2 Mc. 6:24-28).

This speech can easily be imagined as coming from the lips of Jesus as he prepared to make the journey to Jerusalem with his apprehensive disciples. Such an expression of fidelity to the will of his Father would naturally evoke a spontaneous reaction from Thomas. "Let us go too, and die with him" (Jn. 11:16). As long as they could not talk Jesus out of making the journey, they would go with him. They seemed to draw strength from his conviction and determination. They would find solace in a verse from one of the Psalms of Ascent. "Those who trust in Yahweh are like Mount Zion, unshakable, standing for ever" (Ps. 125:1).

As they made their way, it became more and more apparent that this journey would not be cloaked in secrecy nor anonymity. They were to accompany Jesus into the holy city in a manner consistent with his vision. Before making the final approach, Jesus sent his disciples off with orders to borrow a donkey for him to use. He was not to enter the City of David on foot, but mounted on a colt, as was befitting David's heir. Although he had made the pilgrimage to Jerusalem many times before, this particular journey was to have special significance for him. He was coming home: laying claim to the city of his ancestor David and entering the Temple, his Father's house. Only later would his followers come to understand the full significance of this event. "This took place to fulfill the prophecy: Say to the daughter of Zion: Look, your king comes to you; he is humble, he rides on a donkey and on a colt, the foal of a beast of burden" (Mt. 21:4-5).

Seeing that Jesus showed no sign of sneaking into Jerusalem nor demonstrated any fear of being recognized, the apostles put aside their feelings of apprehension. Seeing Jesus seated upon the donkey, they were caught up in the emotion of the moment. "The crowds of people spread their cloaks on the road, while others were cutting branches from trees and spreading them in his path. The crowds who went in front of him and those who followed were all shouting: 'Hosanna to the Son of David! Blessings on him who comes in the name of the Lord! Hosanna in the highest heavens!'" (Mt. 21:8-9). While the common folk hastened to take up the theme, the leaders and members of the ruling body of Jerusalem were opposed to such a demonstration, especially during these solemn days. The people rushed out to greet the bridegroom, while their leaders demurred, preferring the darkness to the Light of Life.

After their sin, unlettered Adam and Eve felt shame and hid themselves when they heard the sound of God's steps coming toward them. The priests, scribes, and Pharisees, who had studied the Law, not only did not hear the approach of their God, but actually took steps to hinder his approach. No longer do sinners hide behind trees or clothe themselves in fig leaves; now they boldly block the path of the Holy One and refuse to allow him access to his holy city. Like his Father, Jesus cried out to the ones he loved, who had hidden themselves from his sight. "Jerusalem, Jerusalem, you that kill the prophets and stone those who are sent to you! How often have I longed to gather your children, as a hen gathers her brood under her wings, and yet you refused! So be it!" (Lk. 13:34).

And yet, while sophisticated adults did not recognize the God of their salvation, simple children ran out to greet him. Loudly did the children sing, "Hosanna to the Son of David! Blessed is he who comes in the name of the Lord" (Mt. 21:8-9). When we compare the response of the adults with that of the children, is it any wonder that Jesus told his disciples that they must become like little children if they wish to enter into the kingdom of heaven? The innocent child is still able to hear the footsteps of God with the ears of his heart.

It is impossible to know exactly how many people had made the pilgrimage, but there is reason to believe that the number was very great. It is clear that people from near and far had come to Jerusalem with the intention of fulfilling the ordinances laid down by Moses concerning the feasts of assembly. Likewise, they had come to reaffirm their faith in Yahweh, the God of all Creation who had brought them out of bondage. The Temple of Jerusalem was the focal point of worship and of their profession of faith.

Had it been necessary for the pilgrims to bring sacrificial victims along with them, the needs of the animals would be nearly impossible to satisfy in the course of the journey. If suitable sacrifices were to be offered, then, appropriate provisions would have to be made in Jerusalem. Realizing this, the Temple officials provided a place where the pilgrims could purchase paschal lambs and other votive offerings. Seen in this light, those who were selling sacrificial victims on the Temple grounds were not desecrating the Holy Place, and Jesus' demonstration at the Temple would have no doubt provoked a sense of dismay and confusion in the minds of the travelers who had come to Jerusalem for the feast. "In the Temple he found people selling cattle and sheep and pigeons, and the money changers sitting at their counters. Making a whip out of some cord, he drove them out of the Temple, cattle and sheep as well, scattered the money changers' coins, knocked their tables over and said to the pigeon sellers, 'Take all this out of here and stop turning my Father's house into a market'" (Jn. 2:13-16). "Nor would he allow anyone to carry anything through the Temple. And he taught them and said, 'Does not Scripture say: My house will be called a house of prayer for all the peoples? But you have turned it into a robbers' den'" (Mk. 11:16-17).

Accounts of Jesus' triumphal entry, which crowned his final pilgrimage to Jerusalem, tell of the enthusiasm of the crowds who went out to greet him. Many took up the cry of "Hosanna!" which is a plea for deliverance. Based on the miracles he had performed and his authoritative preaching, there was agreement that he was a wonder worker and a visionary. Many were ready to acclaim him Messiah—"God's Anointed." However, the meaning of this term was not clear; each faction understood it in a different way. The Pharisees, members of a reform movement which was strong in the synagogue setting but not among the Temple authorities, were at odds with the Sadducees, the priests who dominated the Temple cult. In the countryside were communities of Essenes, a somewhat radical and esoteric sect that was opposed to the Temple establishment. Finally there were the militant Zealots, whose main objective was the overthrow of Roman rule. Each party had its own messianic hope: the Pharisees wanted a learned teacher; the Sadducees hoped for a priestly king; the Essenes looked for a mystic or enlightened leader, a prophet, who would usher in a new age; and the Zealots were awaiting the arrival of a charismatic warrior who would liberate them.

Certainly the sight of Jesus seated upon the colt and riding into Jerusalem amid cries of acclamation excited the messianic hopes of many. Some may have had visions of the Maccabean revolt, expecting Jesus to march on the Roman garrison. How shocked they must have been when he dismounted only to disrupt the sales of votive offerings in the Temple precincts! People had traveled a great distance to keep the Passover; if there were no sacrificial offerings available, how were they to fulfill their obligations? Of course, this was not the first time Jesus had questioned assumptions concerning the sacrificial system. Consider the encounter between Jesus and a scribe which is recorded in Mark's gospel.

> The scribe said to him, "Well spoken, Master; what you have said is true: that he is one and there is no other. To love him with all your heart, with all your understanding and strength, and to love your neighbour as yourself, this is far more important than any holocaust or sacrifice." Jesus, seeing how wisely he had spoken, said, "You are not far from the kingdom of God." And after that no one dared to question him any more (Mk. 12:32-34).

It is possible that Jesus was acting out the insights of the scribe when he cleared the vendors out of the Temple. Jesus, like the prophets of old, was reminding the people that God does not desire the blood of sheep and goats, but rather, hearts overflowing with love for him and for his people. Jesus' demonstration in the Temple can be better understood in light of the comments made to the woman at the well. "Believe me, woman, the hour is coming when you will worship the Father neither on this mountain nor in Jerusalem. You worship what you do not know; we worship what we do know; for salvation comes from the Jews. But the hour will come—in fact it is here already—when true worshipers will worship the Father in spirit and truth: that is the kind of worshiper the Father wants. God is spirit, those who worship must worship in spirit and truth" (Jn. 4:21-24). It is not sacrifice or oblation that the Father wants; he desires the worship of an undivided heart.

The preaching of Jesus concerning "true worship" is deeply rooted in the writings of the prophets. Amos writes, "I hate and despise your feasts, I take no pleasure in your solemn festivals. When you offer me holocausts, I regret your oblations,

and refuse to look at your sacrifices of fattened cattle. Let me
have no more of the din of your chanting, no more of your
strumming on harps. But let justice flow like water and integrity like an unfailing stream" (Am. 5:21-24). In another place we
read, "They love sacrificing; right, let them sacrifice! They love
meat; right, let them eat it! Yahweh takes no pleasure in these.
He is now going to remember their iniquity and punish their
sins; they will have to go back to Egypt" (Hos. 8:13). Yet again
we read, "What is my beloved doing in my house? She is playing the hypocrite! Can vows and consecrated meat rid you of
guilt? Am I to make you clean because of this?" (Jer. 11:15).

Certainly, the pious pilgrims who escorted Jesus into
Jerusalem were not expecting to hear such caustic criticism.
They had endured the hardships of the caravan only to watch
this itinerant preacher disrupt their Passover preparations.
One gets a hint of their confusion and dismay in the questions
put to Jesus by the Temple officials. "The chief priests and the
scribes and the elders came to him, and they said to him,
'What authority have you for acting like this? Or who gave
you authority to do these things?'" (Mk. 11:28). What Jesus had
done was not meant to ingratiate himself to the people. In
accord with the prophetic tradition, his actions were intended
to be provocative. "This is a wicked generation; it is asking for
a sign. The only sign it will be given is the sign of Jonah. For
just as Jonah became a sign to the Ninevites, so will the Son of
Man be to this generation" (Lk. 11:29-30). In John's gospel,
Jesus becomes even more explicit. "Destroy this sanctuary, and
in three days I will raise it up" (Jn. 2:19).

Jesus knew himself to be the herald of the kingdom of God.
He knew himself to be the unique Son through whom the
Father would be glorified. His predictions of the destruction of
the Temple give us some indication of the situation, as he saw
and understood it. The Temple, the sanctuary area, the rites of
sacrifice, and the sacred priesthood were all signs of a faithful
response to God's covenant. The pilgrims had all made a diffi-
cult journey to Jerusalem in order to celebrate the Passover, the
feast which commemorated the loving kindness of God whereby Israel was brought forth from Egypt, the land of slavery.

Motivated by fervor and devotion, they come to the Temple, only to encounter Jesus' symbolic action and to hear his prophetic utterance which prefigured the disintegration of the whole sacrificial system. It seemed that Jesus was striking at the very heart of the Jewish way of life. Rather than encouraging their devotion, Jesus seemed to be hindering it. Uneasy feelings of shock and dismay are suppressed and foment until they find full expression in the accusations brought against Jesus later in the week. The charge of blasphemy is not so much a rational judgment as it is a passionate, almost instinctive, revulsion of feeling against what was perceived as a desecration of that which was held to be sacred.

Not only had Jesus rejected the positions taken by the Essenes and the Zealots, he had also called into question the authority of the Sanhedrin and criticized the teachings and devotional practices of the Pharisees. Finally, he struck at the very heart of the faith of the children of Israel. By expelling the sellers of votive offerings from the Temple precincts and speaking of the destruction of the Temple, he was announcing the end of the Jewish cult. One can only surmise the thoughts of the stunned crowd who had been waiting to make a purchase so as to offer a suitable sacrifice.

We do not find Jesus criticizing the priests for being dishonest, immoral, or corrupt. The sellers are not condemned for unethical sales practices, nor for charging exorbitant fees. He merely drives out the merchants, attempting to close down the sacrifice market. Coupled with his statement concerning the destruction of the Temple, the meaning of the "cleansing of the Temple" becomes clear. Jesus had preached that the kingdom of God was close at hand. He knew himself to be the instrument of its advent. By putting a stop to the sacrifices which were being offered in the Temple, he was predicting the imminent appearance of God's judgment and the coming of the new age. It is not certain if Jesus had himself threatened to destroy the Temple. It was a part of Jewish lore that when the new age would begin, however, the Temple would be cleansed of all defilement and would be replaced by one which would descend from the heavenly realms. This is alluded to in the

Book of Revelation. "In the spirit, he took me to the top of an enormous high mountain and showed me Jerusalem, the holy city, coming down from God out of heaven" (Rv. 21:10).

Whatever Jesus' actual motives for what he did and said in the Temple precincts, his hearers were infuriated. He may have walked away unharmed that day, but his arrest and subsequent execution were quite predictable from that moment on.

> But Shephatiah son of Mattan, Gedaliah son of Pashhur, Jucal son of Shelemiah and Pashhur son of Malchiah heard the words which Jeremiah was saying to all the people. . . . These leading men accordingly spoke to the king. "Let this man be put to death: he is unquestionably disheartening the remaining soldiers in the city, and all the people too, by talking like this. The fellow does not have the welfare of this people at heart so much as its ruin." "He is in your hands as you know," King Zedekiah answered "for the king is powerless against you." So they took Jeremiah and threw him into the well of Prince Malchiah in the Court of the Guard, letting him down with ropes. There was no water in the well, only mud, and into the mud Jeremiah sank (Jer. 38:1, 4-6).

Three

Hatching the Plot

Unearthing the Snake Pit, Laying Bare the Heel of the Son of God

The events of Palm Sunday had set the seal on Jesus' fate. The exuberant crowds which had gathered around Jesus to celebrate his triumphal entry into the city were scandalized by his demonstration in the Temple precincts. The city was already overcrowded due to the great number of pilgrims, making security a problem. Now, the excitement caused by Jesus could only arouse additional concern in the minds of the authorities. This is reflected in the Gospel of Luke. "The chief priests and the scribes were looking for some way of doing away with him, because they mistrusted the people" (Lk. 22:2). This line has always intrigued me. Why would the leaders of pious pilgrims fear them? Were they anxious about losing their moral authority over them? Did they fear the people would take the law into their own hands bringing down Roman reprisals at this holy time?

The travelers had endured the challenges of the caravan journey to be in Jerusalem for the Passover. They had come to fulfill the commands of Moses concerning the offering of the Passover lamb. Like their ancestors of old, they had come before God to celebrate his great act of loving kindness whereby they were brought out of Egypt, the land of slavery. With renewed faith in the God of their salvation, they came to make suitable sacrifice to the Lord. Queuing up at the vendors' stalls, they wait their turn, hoping they will still have time to make all the necessary preparations for lodging and board. They watch Jesus drive the sellers out of the Temple grounds. Then he speaks of the destruction of the Temple and calls upon the faithful people to offer the sacrifice which the Father really wants: a sacrifice offered in spirit and truth. This could be interpreted to mean that the journey was not really necessary; they might have done better to stay home and demonstrate their love of God by loving their neighbor, a sacrifice which is more pleasing to God than the smell of burning victims.

It is one thing to discuss the fine points of Torah and Talmud with the learned, quite another to disrupt the anxious activity of the Passover preparations. The travelers are tired and worn out by the rigors of the caravan; they are nearing the deadline for procuring the paschal lamb. With the passage of time, people would naturally start pushing and getting disagreeable. Jesus' prophetic gesture came at a time when the people were already mentally and physically harassed. Holy man or not, his actions could not have been received with equanimity. Judging how volatile the situation had become, the Temple officials knew they had to intervene before the Romans could move in and impose "peace." "One of them, Caiaphas, the high priest that year, said, 'You don't seem to have grasped the situation at all; you fail to see that it is better for one man to die for the people, than for the whole nation to be destroyed'" (Jn. 11:49-50).

If Jesus were not silenced and removed from the scene, no one could be certain what measures would be taken by certain elements of the crowd. And if Jesus were murdered, would the vendetta end there? This does not seem to be a far-fetched question. The gospels tell us that this was the fear of the apostles. "In the evening of that same day, the first day of the week, the doors were closed in the room where the disciples were, for fear of the Jews" (Jn. 20:19). If mob action were to begin, the Romans would step in and then there would be no telling how many victims would be left dead. At the same time, they had to be careful because should the Temple guard move in, some people might create an incident, again inviting a response from the Romans. Jesus would have to be taken into custody under the cloak of secrecy in order to avoid needless Roman reprisals.

To stop at this level, however, would be to miss a deeper drama. The course of action presented to the chief priests seemed "good" and "pleasing" to the mind's eye, and even "desirable" for the supposed security it would bring. As we add these few familiar words, we find ourselves standing beneath the tree of knowledge of good and evil. Looking up, we might see the coiled body of the serpent and hear his seductive voice. "No! you will not die! God knows in fact that on the day you eat it your eyes will be opened and you will be like gods knowing good and evil" (Gn. 3:5). In the Garden of Eden, all that God created and declared to be good became an instrument of evil and death, having been tainted by Satan's venom. By blinding the eyes of the mind and deafening the ears of the heart, Satan warps the judgment of human beings, turning them away from the God who made them for himself. By keeping the third chapter of Genesis in mind as we read the passion accounts, we gain new insights into the events of the last week of Christ's life.

"Then Satan entered into Judas, surnamed Iscariot, who was numbered among the Twelve. He went to the chief priests and the officers of the guard to discuss a scheme for handing Jesus over to them. They were delighted and agreed to give him money. He accepted and looked for an opportunity to betray him to them without the people knowing" (Lk. 22:3-6). Volumes have been written on the subject of Judas' reasoning for going to the Temple authorities. Was he, in fact, the traitor tradition has made him out to be? Judas had witnessed the exuberant reception Jesus got at the city gate; he also felt the confusion and rage of the crowd at the Temple. Seeing how volatile the situation had become, could he possibly have been looking for a way to get Jesus out of immediate danger? Perhaps he thought that Jesus would be kept in custody until tempers had cooled and the pilgrims had returned to their homes. He must also have felt that Jesus would taken no pre-cautionary steps on his own. In the interest of Jesus' ministry, someone had to do something; entering into an alliance with the chief priests seemed the best solution.

In trying to understand how Judas could have betrayed Jesus into the hands of the very people who would have him put to death, it might be helpful to consider the story of Joseph who was sold into slavery by his own brothers. Pay special attention to the role of Reuben.

> But Reuben heard, and he saved him from their violence. "We must not take his life," he said. "Shed no blood," said Reuben to them "throw him into this well in the wilderness, but do not lay violent hands on him"—intending to save him from them and to restore him to his father. So, when Joseph reached his brothers, they pulled off his coat with long sleeves that he was wearing, and catching hold of him they threw him into the well, an empty well with no water in it. . . . When Reuben went back to the well there was no sign of Joseph. Tearing his clothes, he went back to his brothers. "The boy has disappeared," he said. "What am I going to do?" (Gn. 37:21-24, 29-30).

Reuben's love and concern for Joseph was not shared by his brothers, neither did the chief priests share Judas' love for Jesus, his Master. As he was hatching his plan of action, Judas had probably hoped his scheme would save Jesus' life. He had no way of knowing how serious the chief priests were in their resolve totally to rid themselves of the threat which Jesus had posed to the Jewish people living under Roman rule. Like Reuben of old, he would soon come to find that his best laid plans were frustrated, and the one whom he had hoped to protect was snatched from him. Events, once set in motion, would take a direction all their own. "They then sat down to eat. Looking up they saw a group of Ishmaelites who were coming from Gilead, their camels laden with gum, tragacanth, balsam and resin, which they were taking down into Egypt. . . . They drew Joseph up out of the well. They sold Joseph to the Ishmaelites for twenty silver pieces, and these men took Joseph to Egypt" (Gn. 37:25, 28).

It seems certain that Judas, like Reuben, did not weigh the

consequences of what he was about to do, nor did he realize the depth of the animosity which the Temple leaders had toward Jesus. Jesus knew what he was about to face and had no naive hopes of saving his own life. He attempted to bring this fact home to his disciples as they shared the Passover supper with him the night before he died. "The Son of Man is going to his fate, as the Scriptures say he will, but alas for the man by whom the Son of Man is betrayed!" (Mk. 14:21). "Having said this, Jesus was troubled in spirit and declared, 'I tell you most solemnly, one of you will betray me.' The disciples looked at one another wondering which he meant" (Jn. 13:21-22). "They were greatly distressed and started asking him in turn, 'Not I, Lord, surely?'" (Mt. 26:22). Even Judas, in his turn, asked this same question.

Jesus understood human nature much better than did Judas. "Jesus knew them all and did not trust himself to them; he never needed evidence about any man; he could tell what a man had in him" (Jn. 2:24-25). As prudently as he could, Jesus tried to warn Judas to be more careful. Unfortunately, Judas was deaf to the words addressed to him and was, therefore, blind to the true implications of his actions. "Jesus dipped the piece of bread and gave it to Judas the son of Simon Iscariot. At that instant, after Judas had taken the bread, Satan entered him. . . . As soon as Judas had taken the piece of bread he went out. Night had fallen" (Jn. 13:26-27, 30). Judas is no longer pictured as walking in the light, but is now wrapped in darkness. He will not come to a realization of the part he is playing in the eternal drama until the two opponents are locked in combat. Only then will he see that the Prince of Darkness had tricked and outwitted him.

"The woman saw that the tree was good to eat and pleasing to the eye, and that it was desirable for the knowledge that it could give. So she took some of its fruit and ate it" (Gn. 3:6). As were our forebears in the garden, so Judas was trapped by Satan's snare. No matter how enticing the course of action, however, the choice, the decision to act, was freely made. Adam, Eve, and Judas could have acted differently. "I kept those you gave me true to our name. I have watched over them and not one is lost except the one who chose to be lost" (Jn. 17:12). Judas chose not to listen to the word of truth and freely acted upon the words of the Tempter. Because of this decision, he unwittingly became part of a scheme which was much bigger than his own. He received a purse of thirty pieces of silver from the chief priests, but the only wage he actually received for his treacherous act was death. "And flinging down the silver pieces in the sanctuary he made off, and went and hanged himself" (Mt. 27:5).

Four

Preparing for the Seder

Everything Must Be Done According to Plan

We have had a glimpse of Judas' preparations for the Passover event. Now we shall turn our attention to Jesus' preparations for his Passover. The scriptures tell us that after having come to Jerusalem, Jesus retired to Bethany. "He looked all about him, but it was now late, he went out to Bethany with the Twelve" (Mk. 11:11). Bethany had figured as an important site of his ministry; now it would be the stage as his final drama unfolded. Bethany was the place "where Lazarus lived, whom he had raised from the dead" (Jn. 12:1). While it is impossible to know what thoughts were running through Jesus' mind, we can presume a few things. Undoubtedly Jesus knew that he had aroused public animosity against himself by his actions and statements in the Temple precincts. Knowing of these heightened emotions, he would also have realized that it would not be wise to stay openly in the city; being a practical man, he would have taken some simple precautions. Thus, during the day, he would preach openly in the Temple; then as evening drew on, he would go to Bethany where he could rest and be secure, for the time being.

We can only imagine the strain Jesus must have been under. Certainly he knew that each and every word was being analyzed; every action was being noted and scrutinized. This was not a time to leave things to chance; every comment and

41

movement must be carefully orchestrated. "Now my soul is troubled. What shall I say: Father, save me from this hour? But it was for this reason that I have come to this hour. Father, glorify your name!" (Jn. 12:27).

No doubt, the cloud which enveloped Jesus also had an effect on his disciples. Upon coming to Jerusalem, they had allowed themselves to be taken up in a triumphal mood, singing and dancing as Jesus sat astride the donkey. Now their worst fears were being confirmed. Despite the fact that they were unwilling to think about the possibility of Jesus' death, they could not get him to stop talking about it. "Then, taking him aside, Peter started to remonstrate with him" (Mk. 8:32). "He said, 'Heaven preserve you, Lord; this must not happen to you.' But Jesus turned and said to Peter, 'Get behind me, Satan! You are an obstacle in my path, because the way you think is not God's way but man's'" (Mt. 16:22-23). As would many who find themselves in such an uncomfortable situation, someone decided to lighten the atmosphere by throwing a party. "They gave a dinner for him; Martha, waited on them and Lazarus was among those at table" (Jn. 12:2).

Although nearly two millennia separate these biblical events from our lives, we can gain some insight into the events of Jesus' passion by reflecting upon the thoughts of Dr. Martin Luther King, Jr., when he was faced with the threat of death.

> On a particular Monday evening, following a tension-packed week which included being arrested and receiving numerous threatening phone calls, I spoke at a mass meeting. I attempted to convey an overt impression of strength and courage, although I was inwardly depressed and fear-stricken. At the end of the meeting, Mother Pollard came to the front of the church and said, "Come here, son." I immediately went to her and hugged her affectionately. "Something is wrong with you," she said. "You didn't talk strong tonight." Seeking further to disguise my fears, I retorted, "Oh, no, Mother Pollard, nothing is wrong. I am feeling as fine as ever." But her insight was discerning. "Now you can't fool me," she said. "I knows something is wrong. Is it that we ain't doing things to please you? Or is it

that the white folks is bothering you?" Before I could respond, she looked directly into my eyes and said, "I done told you we is with you all the way." Then her face became radiant and she said in words of quiet certainty, "But even if we ain't with you, God's gonna take care of you." As she spoke these consoling words, everything in me quivered and quickened with the pulsing tremor of raw energy *(A Testament of Hope).*

Mary of Bethany did for Jesus what Mother Pollard did for Dr. King. "Mary brought in a pound of very costly ointment, pure nard, and with it anointed the feet of Jesus, wiping them with her hair; the house was full of the scent of the ointment" (Jn. 12:3). She knew that her gesture could not change the course of events; at the same time, she refused to stand by and do nothing to ease our Lord's mind. She knew that he was not a man given to histrionics. This wordless gesture would demonstrate her love and support. She anoints his feet, soothing away the effects of the heat of the day, using perfumed ointment so that the scent would linger as a reminder of abiding concern.

This demonstration of feminine kindness has never seemed to square with masculine comprehension. Men are usually uncomfortable whenever such displays of tenderness are made. Luke's gospel records a similar reaction: "If this man were a prophet, he would know who this woman is that is touching him and what a bad name she has" (Lk. 7:39). Luke's "this woman" is not Mary of Bethany, but both women can attest to the fact that such acts towards Jesus were brushed off as being superfluous. His acceptance of such signs of womanly devotion would be construed as a sign of weakness and make him a target of accusations of inconsistency.

The disciples had recently watched Jesus eject the merchants from the Temple area. They had also heard him encouraging works of charity and mercy, quoting the scriptures as valuing them more than the odor of any burnt offering. Now they watch this extravagant display of Mary's affection. "When they saw this, the disciples were indignant; 'Why this waste?' they said. 'This could have been sold at a high price and the money given to the poor'" (Mt. 26:8-9).

Whatever motives lay behind the comment, they must have been surprised when Jesus chided them and praised Mary. "Jesus said, 'Leave her alone. Why are you upsetting her? What she has done for me is one of the good works. You have the poor with you always, and you can be kind to them whenever you wish, but you will not always have me. She has done what was in her power to do; she has anointed my body before its burial'" (Mk. 14:6-8). Even though the disciples were beginning to gain insight into some of Jesus' teachings, he did not want them to lose sight of the fact that he was about to die. Throughout his ministry, the disciples had refused to listen to his comments about death. Now, his pungent words were intensified by the aroma of the ointment.

The power of the moment is captured in a reflection shared by Dr. King.

> I had invited the audience to join me in prayer, and had begun by asking God's guidance and direction in all our activities. Then, in the grip of an emotion I could not control, I said, "Lord, I hope no one will have to die as a result of our struggle for freedom in Montgomery. Certainly I don't want to die. But if anyone has to die, let it be me." The audience was in an uproar. Shouts and cries of "No! No!" came from all sides. So intense was the reaction that I could not go on with my prayer. Two of my fellow ministers came to the pulpit and suggested that I take a seat. For a few minutes I stood there with their arms around me, unable to move. Finally, with the help of my friends, I sat down (*A Testament of Hope*).

The statements are simple and straightforward. The words are wrought with emotions and the reaction of the audience is filled with love and anxiety. There is to be no simplistic short-sightedness, nor false hope offered. We have a context wherein to understand the words of Jesus: "I have told you this now before it happens, so that when it does happen you may believe" (Jn. 14:29).

It is important, having considered such emotion-filled

moments that we avoid a portrayal of Jesus as a melancholy, Hamlet-like character. Although he does not go to his crucifixion with spirited enthusiasm, he is, nonetheless, never a hapless victim of some political machine. Although somber, he always holds to an unflagging confidence in the Father, knowing himself to be the special agent whereby the kingdom will be established. Live or die, the victory will be God's. Jesus wants his disciples to have this same confidence, no matter what they will see happening to him in the following days.

"On the first day of Unleavened Bread, when the Passover lamb was sacrificed, his disciples said to him, 'Where do you want us to go and make preparations for you to eat the Passover?'" (Mk. 14:12). But what was the nature of the preparations to be made and the Passover to be celebrated? We might gain some insights from the story of Isaac. "It happened some time later that God put Abraham to the test. 'Abraham, Abraham,' he called. 'Here I am,' he replied. 'Take your son,' God said, 'your only child Isaac, whom you love, and go to the land of Moriah. There you shall offer him as a burnt offering, on a mountain I will point out to you'" (Gn. 22:1-2). The servant of God must be willing to set out, not knowing where the journey will lead. The fruit of knowledge is withheld and the disciples must follow the instructions given them along the way.

> Jesus sent two of his disciples, saying to them, "Go into the city and you will meet a man carrying a pitcher of water. Follow him, and say to the owner of the house which he enters, 'The Master says: Where is my dining room in which I can eat the passover with my disciples?' He will show you a large upper room furnished with couches, all prepared. Make the preparations for us there." The disciples set out and went to the city and found everything as he had told them, and prepared the Passover (Mk. 14:13-16).

"Isaac spoke to his father Abraham, 'Father' he said. 'Yes, my son' he replied. 'Look,' he said 'here are the fire and the wood, but where is the lamb for the burnt offering?' Abraham answered, 'My son, God himself will provide the lamb for the burnt offering.' Then the two of them went on together" (Gn.

22:7-8). Everyone knows how the story of Isaac ends: after the child had been bound and prepared for sacrifice, God intervened and provided the lamb of sacrifice. At this Supper, Jesus gives a new interpretation to the bread of suffering and the cup of blessing. No longer were they reminders of the feast of liberation from Egypt; from this time forward, they were to be served at the wedding banquet of the Lamb of God, who was to be slain.

Five

The Passover Feast

Wisdom Has Set the Table

It is no coincidence that the passion of the Lord Jesus Christ took place within the context of the Passover festival. The going forth from Bethany is closely related to the going forth from Egypt and the going forth from Paradise. Each is done in conformity with God's salvific will and plan for the whole human race. To separate the passion of Christ from the Genesis event or from the Exodus event is to miss the impact of all that God had promised to bring about through the Son. The serpent will strike the Son's heel, but the Son will crush the serpent's head. Soon the Son of Man would be raised up on the tree so that the glory of God might be made manifest. The passion accounts are filled with the notion of time as moving according to a preconceived plan. "When the hour came, Jesus took his place at table, and the apostles with him" (Lk. 22:14).

The notion of "fullness of time" or "the hour" would prove central to salvation history.

> At various times in the past and in various different ways, God spoke to our ancestors through the prophets; but now, in our own time, the last days, he has spoken to us through his Son, the Son that he has appointed to inherit everything and through whom he made everything there is. He is the radiant light of God's glory and the perfect copy of his nature, sustaining the universe by his powerful command; and now

that he has destroyed the defilement of sin, he has gone
to take his place in heaven at the right hand of the
divine Majesty (Heb. 1:1-3).

Jesus was a man with a mission to accomplish. He was fully
aware of the dangers which it entailed, but it was for this that
he was born. For him, there could be no turning back, no other
way. "Everyone who comes to me and listens to my words and
acts on them—I will tell you what he is like. He is like the man
who when he built his house dug, and dug deep, and laid the
foundation on rock; when the river was in flood it bore down
on that house but could not shake it, it was so well built" (Lk.
6:47-48). Jesus was grounded on the vision he had received
from the Father; he would not be shaken by the flood waters
which were rising around his neck. "Once the hand is laid on
the plough, no one who looks back is fit for the kingdom of
God" (Lk. 9:62). The labor undertaken in the heat of the day is
grueling and saps the body of strength, but the Lord knew that
he must labor on and not look back, nor count the cost. This
commitment to the fulfillment would be repeated in the letters
of Paul. "I can assure you my brothers, I am far from thinking
I have already won. All I can say is that I forget the past and
strain ahead for what is still to come; I am racing for the finish,
for the prize to which God calls us upwards to receive in
Christ Jesus" (Phil. 3:13-14).

Jesus knew that his role in the history of the people of Israel
was rooted in the very promises made to Moses at Sinai. He
came to Jerusalem to celebrate the feast of Passover, just as he
had done many times in the past; yet he knew that this particular Passover was to be quite different from any other. He
entered the holy city in the company of devout pilgrims,
whereupon he cleansed the Temple of the sacrifice sellers,
demonstrating the end of Temple sacrifice and the dawning of
a new age. Similarly, the Passover supper would begin with
the ancient rites concerning the sacrificial lamb of the old
covenant. The old ritual completed, a new rite would be initiated marking the establishment of a new covenant which
would be ratified in the blood of the Lamb of God.

We have no way of knowing the exact ritual followed by

Jesus and his disciples in the upper room. It is not certain whether it followed the form of the Seder used by the Jewish communities in our time, and we have no relevant manuscripts from that period. We can, however, piece together some of the dialogue by reading the passages from the Old Testament and by gleaning the fragmentary comments contained in the gospel accounts. There are some simple phrases in the preaching of Jesus and in the letters of Paul which find expression in the Passover ritual in the form it has today.

Mark's gospel says, "Then he gave them this warning, 'Keep your eyes open; be on your guard against the yeast of the Pharisees and the yeast of Herod'" (Mk. 8:15). Then, in Paul: "So get rid of all the old yeast, and make yourselves into a completely new batch of bread, unleavened as you are meant to be. Christ, our Passover, has been sacrificed; let us celebrate the feast, then, by getting rid of all the old yeast of evil and wickedness, having only the unleavened bread of sincerity and truth" (1 Cor. 5:7-8). According to the ritual of the Passover, the house where the Seder was to be held had to be thoroughly leaven-free. Only after the house had been inspected and certified to be free of all leaven and yeast could the supper begin. And so, once the disciples were free from yeast—the yeast of the Pharisees and sin—and after they had clothed themselves in sincerity and truth, they sat in expectation of the setting sun, which heralded the coming of a new day.

Only when the sun had set and the first star of evening appeared could the true Light of the World be made known. The Passover ritual contains this traditional prayer for the lighting of the festal lights: "Blessed are you, Lord our God, King of the Universe, who has sanctified us by your commandments and commanded us to kindle the festival lights. May our gathering be consecrated, O God, by the light of your countenance, shining upon us in blessing and peace" (*The Passover Haggadah*).

The lighting of the festal lights evokes memories of the desire voiced by Jesus in Luke's gospel. "I have come to bring fire to the earth, and how I wish it were blazing already!" (Lk. 12:49). Having seen the light enkindled, Peter could write:

"You are a chosen race, a royal priesthood, a consecrated nation, a people set apart to sing the praises of God who called you out of the darkness into his wonderful light" (1 Pt. 2:9).

Peter knew, though, that this moment of light would not come without pain. Before the feast was over, he would see an innocent and holy man condemned and crucified by the Romans; a trusted friend would turn traitor; he himself would deny his Master, as he watched all his hopes dashed to the ground in utter defeat.

Throughout the Seder, Jesus would make certain modifications in the ceremony. These changes no doubt had a pronounced impact on the disciples, not unlike the effect of the cleansing of the Temple. It was customary, for example, for the head of the house to wash his hands at table before the actual meal began. However, on this night Jesus did something quite different. "He knew that the Father had put everything into his hands, and that he had come from God and was returning to God, and he got up from the table, removed his outer garment and, taking a towel, wrapped it round his waist; he then poured water into a basin and began to wash the disciples' feet and to wipe them with the towel he was wearing" (Jn. 13:3-5).

Jesus knew that he had his disciples' attention; being the good teacher, he now proceeded to impress on them the full meaning of his teaching. "The greatest among you must be your servant. Anyone who exalts himself will be humbled, and anyone who humbles himself will be exalted" (Mt. 23:11-12). Jesus' actions were to serve as a demonstration of his gospel. "When he had washed their feet and put on his clothes again he went back to the table. 'Do you understand,' he said, 'what I have done to you? You call me "Master" and "Lord," and rightly: so I am. If I, then, the Lord and Master, have washed your feet, you should wash each other's feet. I have given you an example so that you may copy what I have done to you'" (Jn. 13:12-15).

We learn along with Jesus' disciples. Jesus, the Word Incarnate, is the full expression of the mind of the Father. To learn the works of the Father, we must follow the example of the Son. "As Scripture says: Who can know the mind of the

Lord, so who can teach him? But we are those who have the mind of Christ" (1 Cor. 2:16). The mind of God is found in the commands which he entrusted to his holy people. "This is my commandment: love one another, as I have loved you" (Jn. 15:12). It is the mind of God that we not only come to the Temple to offer sacrifice, but that we sacrifice ourselves in the service of those who are in need.

During the meal, Jesus took bread, broke it, and recited the ritual blessing. "Blessed are you, eternal our God, Ruler of the Universe, who brings forth bread from the earth, and commanded us concerning the eating of unleavened bread." Here, again, Jesus reshaped the ritual of the seder and reinterpreted the meaning of the bread. "Take it and eat; this is my body" (Mt. 26:26). Earlier in his ministry, Jesus had spoken of himself as "bread." "I am the bread of life. He who comes to me will never be hungry; he who believes in me will never thirst" (Jn. 6:34). By giving this new meaning to the Passover bread, Jesus was telling his disciples that his words were not to be taken symbolically.

Jesus, likewise, took the cup of wine and offered the ritual blessing: "Blessed are you, eternal our God, Ruler of the Universe, Creator of the fruit of the vine." Having fulfilled the formal ritual of the seder, Jesus then gives a new interpretation to the cup of blessing: "Drink all of you from this, for this is my blood, the blood of the new covenant, which is to be poured out for many for the forgiveness of sins" (Mt. 26:28). Here, it is important to call to mind another of Jesus' previous comments. "For my flesh is real food and my blood is real drink. He who eats my flesh and drinks my blood lives in me and I live in him" (Jn. 6:55-56). In the New Covenant we are not just members of the chosen people, we are made one with the One who called us, and thus we are transformed into the very holiness of the One who is Holy.

St. Paul offers further insight into the seder of the new covenant.

> For this is what I received from the Lord, and in turn passed on to you: that on the same night that he was betrayed, the Lord Jesus took some bread, and thanked

God for it and broke it, and he said, "This is my body, which is for you; do this as a memorial of me." In the same way he took the cup after supper and said, "This cup is the covenant in my blood. Whenever you drink it, do this as a memorial of me." Until the Lord comes, therefore, every time you eat this bread and drink this cup, you are proclaiming his death, and so anyone who eats the bread and drinks the cup of the Lord unworthily will be behaving unworthily towards the body and blood of the Lord (1 Cor. 11:23-27).

The Passover of the Jews marks the deliverance of God's chosen people from Egypt, the land of slavery; the Passover of Jesus marks the deliverance of the children of God from sin and death. Jesus takes the bread and wine of the first Passover and transforms it into the memorial of the second. Once the bread was blessed and broken, once the wine was blessed and poured out, the Lord Jesus was truly present to his disciples. "Now while he was with them at table, he took the bread and said the blessing; then he broke it and handed it to them. And their eyes were opened and they recognized him; but he had vanished from their sight. Then they said to each other, 'Did not our hearts burn within us as he talked to us on the road and explained the Scriptures to us?'" (Lk. 24:30-32).

We, too, encounter Jesus in the bread and wine. For nearly two millennia Christians have been gathering around the holy table to hear the word of scripture broken open for them and to partake of the banquet of the Lamb. There is a beautiful prayer in the Latin liturgy, prayed by the priest just before communion, which suggests the meaning of our own participation in this meal: "Lord Jesus Christ, Son of the living God, by the will of the Father and the work of the Holy Spirit your death had brought life to the world. By your holy Body and Blood, free me from all my sins and from every evil. Keep me faithful to your teaching, and never let me be parted from you."

Jesus was the instrument of the coming of the kingdom. His prayerful insights had led him to realize that the kingdom would only come after his agonizing death. After the celebration of the Passover at which he had given the disciples the new interpretations of the bread and cup, he also opened their eyes to the reality of the price which would be exacted. "And Jesus said to them, 'You will lose faith, for the scriptures say: I shall strike the shepherd and the sheep will scatter, however, after my resurrection I shall go before you to Galilee'" (Mk. 14:27-28). To be a follower of Jesus, we too must be willing to enter into the "black hole" of the crucifixion with its accompanying suffering, pain, and apparent defeat. We must be willing to face despair and abandonment. It is through death that we come to the newness of life which is realized in the resurrection.

"Simon, Simon! Satan, you must know, has got his wish to sift you all like wheat; but I have prayed for you, Simon, that your faith may not fail, and once you have recovered, you in your turn must strengthen your brothers" (Lk. 22:31-32). Jesus looks at his disciples and tells them that the glory of God is not found in strength and power. If they are to experience the resurrection, they must be willing to fall, to feel the pain of defeat and then allow the power from on high to lift them up so as to be able to give support to others in need. "After he had said all this Jesus left with his disciples and crossed the Kedron valley. There was a garden there, and he went into it with his disciples" (Jn. 18:1).

Six

The Garden of Gethsemane
A Time of Testing

Because so much stress is placed upon the week of Jesus' passion, we might be tempted to think that this Passover pilgrimage and celebration was unique in his life. The gospels tell us, however, that Jesus was accustomed to going to Jerusalem for the feast. Likewise, they tell us that Jesus was accustomed to spending time away from the crowd in the Garden of Gethsemane. "Judas the traitor knew the place well since Jesus had often met his disciples there" (Jn. 10:2). Throughout his ministry, Jesus would seek out places of solitude where he could spend long periods in communion with his Father. "In the morning, long before dawn, he got up and left the house, and went off to a lonely place and prayed there" (Mk. 1:35). Such behavior was usual for Jesus, as demonstrated in another passage from Mark's gospel: "After saying good-bye to them he went off into the hills to pray" (Mk. 6:46). Not only was Jesus a holy man, he was known to be one who prayed. He took his disciples with him so that they could learn to be people of prayer by following his example. Jesus would begin his mission in the desert and would spend the last night of his life in the garden: his ministry began in a desolate place and it ended in desolation and interior anguish.

"Filled with the Holy Spirit, Jesus left the Jordan and was led by the Spirit through the wilderness, being tempted there by the devil for forty days" (Lk. 4:1-2). Wandering the wilderness, aided only by his vision and guided only by the will of his Father, Jesus had no physical resources to support him: the scriptures tell us that he had fasted for forty days and experienced great weakness. It is now that he is tempted by the Evil One, confronted by the infernal Serpent, and that he manifests his purity of heart. During that first venture into the desert solitude, Jesus hears the question: "Are you the Son of God?" After John the Baptist is arrested and Jesus begins his ministry, he is questioned by disciples of John who ask: "Are you the One who is to come, or must we wait for someone else?"

Now, on the night before his death, Jesus enters into the olive grove and experiences the weight of the press coming down upon him. He knew that the hour had come and that he could not turn back. "But this is your hour; this is the reign of darkness" (Lk. 22:53). The scriptures tell us that Jesus was filled with distress. It is not possible for us to fathom the depths of this desolation, a desolation which would find its full expression in the words: "My God, why have you forsaken me?" We cannot begin to identify with the feelings of the Light of the World who finds himself enveloped by complete and total darkness. "The lamp of the body is the eye. It follows that if your eye is sound, your whole body will be filled with light. But if your eye is diseased, your whole body will be all darkness. If then, the light inside you is darkness, what darkness that will be!" (Mt. 6:22-23). The darkness that the Light must have felt finds expression in the words of Jesus. "My soul is sorrowful to the point of death" (Mk. 14:34).

As the obedience of our forebears, Adam and Eve, was tried in the garden, so now the obedience of the Son of the Woman is put to the test in the Garden of Gethsemane. After his baptism in the Jordan, Jesus confronted Satan in the solitude of the wilderness, weakened by fasting but sustained by the anointing of the Holy Spirit. This night, however, Jesus faces Satan in the solitude of the garden, strengthened by the meal which he has just eaten, but totally devoid of consolation either from friend or Spirit. The hour had come. Now the kingdom of the Father would be made manifest; the light would shine forth for all to see. But first, the Prince of Darkness must be forced to manifest himself for what he truly is. The darkness of sin and death must be overcome by the light of truth and life.

Jesus enters into the garden and is overwhelmed by his vulnerable condition. He has just eaten the Paschal feast, celebrating the deliverance of his people from Egypt, that land of slavery. Knowing that he is to set his people free from the tyranny of sin and death, he now separates himself from all human comfort and physical signs of assurance. This stripping of self reminds us of David preparing to face Goliath: "Saul made David put on his own armour and put a bronze helmet on his head and gave him a breast plate to wear, and over David's armour he buckled his own sword; but not being used to these things David found he could not walk. 'I cannot walk with these,' he said to Saul 'I am not used to them.' So he took them off again" (1 Sam. 17:38-39). Naked, and divested of all means of physical protection or human comfort, Jesus is to fulfill the Father's will for the salvation of the world. No one and nothing is to stand between him and his infernal adversary. He is to leave himself completely vulnerable so that the glory of the Father might be made manifest through him.

The gospels paint the picture for us, one almost as graphic as that of David preparing to meet Goliath. "And Jesus said to his disciples, 'Stay here while I pray.' Then he took Peter and James and John with him. . . . And going a little further he threw himself on the ground and prayed" (Mk. 14:32-33, 35). Jesus knew that he was the unique Son of God, and that he was also the Son of the Woman who was to bring about the kingdom of the Father. He also knew that he alone was to walk this pilgrimage through the valley of death. Despite the feeling of human revulsion at the thought of suffering and tortuous death, Jesus was committed to fulfilling the Father's plan. We might gain some insight into Jesus' attitude by reading the complaint of Jeremiah the prophet.

> You have seduced me, Yahweh, and I have let myself be seduced; you have overpowered me: you were the stronger. I am a daily laughing-stock, everybody's butt. Each time I speak the word, I have to howl and proclaim:

"Violence and ruin!" The word of Yahweh has meant for me insult, derision, all day long. I used to say, "I will not think about him, I will not speak in his name any more." Then there seemed to be a fire burning in my heart, imprisoned in my bones. The effort to restrain it wearied me. I could not bear it (Jer. 20:7-9).

This concept of having to release the word once it has taken hold of the messenger is presented in the Book of Job. "For I am filled with words, choked by the rush of them within me. I have a feeling in my heart like new wine seeking a vent, and bursting a brand new wineskin. Nothing will bring relief but speech, I will open my mouth and give my answer" (Jb. 32:18-29). Jesus is overwhelmed by the desolation which fills his soul and, like Job and Jeremiah, he does not remain silent. "In his anguish he prayed even more earnestly, and his sweat fell to the ground like great drops of blood" (Lk. 22:44).

Remember that Jesus came into this world to be our *goel* in the battle against Satan. Jesus' agony in the garden is not merely an emotional reaction to his impending execution. In the shadows lurks the Prince of Darkness; now is his hour.

So Yahweh said to Satan, "Where have you been?" "Round the earth," he answered, "roaming about." So Yahweh asked him, "Did you notice my servant Job? There is no one like him on the earth: a sound and honest man who fears God and shuns evil. His life continues to be blameless as ever; in vain you provoked me to ruin him." "A skin is fair exchange for a skin!" Satan replied. "A man will give away all he has to save his life. But stretch out your hand and lay a finger on his bone and flesh; I warrant you, he will curse you to your face." "Very well," Yahweh said to Satan "he is in your power" (Jb. 2:2-7).

At long last, the Serpent and the offspring of the woman confront each other. They had spared with each other once before, but this would be the final conflict. The two opponents are about to engage each other in a fight to the death. As we reflect on the three temptations, we gain important insights into this conflict. "Satan led him to Jerusalem and made him stand on the parapet of the Temple. 'If you are the Son of God,' he said to him 'throw yourself down from here, for scripture says: he will put his angels in charge of you to guard you'" (Lk. 4:9-10). Would Satan have mocked Jesus' cowardice and chided him for having a weak will? Then, knowing Jesus' mortal anguish, would he have played upon Jesus' weakened state in hopes of making him curse God? This night, Satan would not take Jesus to the Temple; rather, he would show him the pillory and give him a foretaste of how the Romans would make sport of one who claimed to be the Son of God. The words which come forth from his lips are not curses. "My Father, if it is possible, let this cup pass me by. Nevertheless, let it be as you, not I, would have it" (Mt. 26:39).

"Then leading him to a height, the devil showed him in a moment of time all the kingdoms of the world and said to him, 'I will give you all this power and the glory of these kingdoms, for it has been committed to me and I give it to anyone I choose. Worship me, then it shall all be yours'" (Lk. 4:5-7). Looking out over the whole universe, Jesus saw but one kingdom, a kingdom which he had spoken of throughout his ministry. "Set your hearts on his kingdom first, and on his righteousness, and all these other things will be given you as well. So do not worry about tomorrow: tomorrow will take care of itself. Each day has enough trouble of its own" (Mt. 6:33-34).

Satan certainly would have pointed out to Jesus his sorry state. A few feet away, his faithful band was sound asleep; off in the distance Judas was guiding a detachment of the Temple guard toward its victim. It was a presage of what tomorrow would bring: a bloody mass of lacerated flesh being cut from the pillar, wrapped in a filthy scarlet rag and crowned with a thorny crown. A sigh comes from Jesus' lips as he recognizes the frame as his own. "Father, if you are willing, take this cup away from me. Nevertheless, let your will be done, not mine" (Lk. 22:42).

After the forty-day fast in the wilderness, Jesus was hungry. The devil had hoped to play upon Jesus' weakness and prod him to misuse his powers for selfish ends. "And the tempter came and said to him, 'If you are the Son of God, tell these stones to turn into loaves'" (Mt. 4:3). Jesus had become one of countless millions who go to bed overcome by physical hunger every night. Yet Jesus also felt a spiritual hunger which gnawed at his very soul. The psalmist writes of such a spiritual languishing. "I am like water draining away, my bones are all disjointed, my heart is like wax, melting inside me; my palate is drier than a potsherd and my tongue is stuck to my jaw" (Ps. 22:14-15). The scene before his eyes is the top of Calvary. Jesus sees himself nailed to the cross, his body throbbing with pain; he is so weak that he cannot lift his head, his lungs bursting, unable to expel the air they contain. Dehydrated from the loss of blood and physical distress caused by the very act of hanging on the cross, he cries out, "I am thirsty" (Jn. 19:28).

The remedy for Adam and Eve's disobedience is the obedience of Jesus. The lie of Satan—"You will not die"—is laid bare by the graphic image of a man tortured, mocked and crucified; his strength is sapped and life drips from his lacerated flesh. For Jesus there would be no tasty morsel to savor; in his nakedness he would be the butt of mockery and derision. There would be no familiar footsteps coming towards him in the cool of the afternoon, only desolation and complete abandonment. Knowing all this, however, Jesus does not shrink from his intended task.

"Then Jesus replied, 'Be off, Satan!'" (Mt. 4:10). "You are an obstacle in my path, because the way you think is not God's" (Mt. 16:23). Overwhelmed and distressed by what he has seen, Jesus again prays to the Father. "My Father, if this cup cannot pass by without my drinking it, your will be done!" (Mt. 26:42). Having abandoned himself totally to the Father's will, Jesus feels no lifting of his spirits, no comfort or consolation. There, in desolation and anguish, he pours out his soul and God is silent. "I had hoped for sympathy, but in vain, I found no one to console me" (Ps. 69:20). No one comes to wipe his sweat-covered brow; no one offers to quiet his troubled thoughts; no one appears to ease his agony. The Light of the World is submerged in darkness, and there he chooses to remain. This experience of Jesus and his fidelity to his Father's will is the central theme of the earliest records of Christian preaching. "During his life on earth, he offered up prayer and entreaty, aloud and in silent tears, to the one who had the power to save him out of death, and he submitted so humbly that his prayer was heard. Although he was Son, he learnt to obey through suffering; and having been made perfect, he became for all who obey him the source of eternal salvation" (Heb. 5:7-9). From the depths of his poverty, we are rich, becoming heirs of the kingdom.

"When he rose from prayer he went to the disciples and found them sleeping" (Lk. 22:45). He roused them and went forth to face his fate. "Now the hour has come when the Son of Man is to be betrayed into the hands of sinners. Get up! Let us go! My betrayer is already close at hand" (Mt. 26:45-46).

T. S. Eliot has Thomas Becket deliver these lines in his sermon for Christmas a few days before his murder in the cathedral: "A Christian martyrdom is never an accident, for saints are not made by accident. Still less is a Christian martyrdom the effect of a man's will to become a saint, as a man by willing and contriving may become a ruler of men. A martyrdom is always the design of God, for his love of men, to warn them and to lead them back to his ways" *(Murder in the Cathedral)*. As the Knights enter the church, Thomas will refuse to bar the doors. With these words he goes to his fate. "The church is not a fortress of oak and stone. We conquer by suffering" *(Murder in the Cathedral)*.

Seven

The Arrest

A Betrayer's Kiss, a Lover's Surrender

In the Byzantine liturgy for Holy Week, we find a hymn which compares Judas with the Hebrew slaves who complained against Moses and God as they ate the manna in the wilderness:

> Truly, Judas is the son of those ungrateful who ate the manna in the wilderness and murmured against the Nourisher; for, while the food was still in their mouths, those ingrates murmured against God. Likewise the wicked one, while the Holy Bread was still in his mouth, conspired to betray the Savior. O what greedy purpose! What bold inhumanity! For he betrayed the Nourisher and delivered to death the Master who loved him. Save our souls, O Lord, from such unkindness; for you alone can endure such long-suffering (Tropar of Holy Thursday).

The hours of waiting are now over. Jesus willingly walks into the trap which has been set by his enemy. The bait is a disciple, a trusted friend, who himself will soon learn that he has been used as a pawn. Jesus sees the torches; he feels the warmth of Judas' lips on his cheek and knows the truth of the visions of the night. The sorrow of his heart finds expression in the words of the psalmist: "Sorrow and misery live inside, ruin is an inmate; tyranny and treachery are never absent from its central square. Were it an enemy who insulted me, I could put up with that; had a rival got the better of me, I could hide from him. But you, a man of my own rank, a colleague and a friend, to whom sweet conversation bound me in the House of God!" (Ps. 55:11-14).

Jesus knew that his life was in danger, yet he chose to do those things which he had always done. He had no intention of altering his ordinary course of actions, even though he knew that he would be extremely vulnerable. It was customary for Jesus to spend the night in the Garden of Gethsemane whenever he came to Jerusalem: the disciples saw nothing unusual in his behavior, and perhaps this is why they fell asleep while he prayed. The solitude was interrupted by the arrival of the Temple guard. "He was still speaking when a number of men appeared, and at the head of them the man called Judas, one of the Twelve, who went up to Jesus to kiss him" (Lk. 22:47). Judas knew exactly where to go and where to find Jesus because he had been there so many times before. This would not be the first time that someone sought Jesus while he was in prayer. "Simon and his companions set out in search of him, and when they found him they said, 'Everybody is looking for you'" (Mk. 1:36-37). In those earlier days, people sought Jesus, wanting to hear his word and find life, but on this night they ignored his words, intending to take his life.

"Knowing everything that was going to happen to him, Jesus then came forward and said, 'Who are you looking for?' they answered, 'Jesus the Nazarene!' He said, 'I am he.' Now Judas the traitor was standing among them" (Jn. 10:4-5). Jesus is no hapless victim of some unjust system; he freely goes out to meet his opponent—not Judas, not the Jews, but Satan. "If I am the one you are looking for, let these others go" (Jn. 18:8). This night, there was to be no mistake, no confusion. Jesus was the *goel*, the champion of his people. He alone would redeem the human race from the clutches of sin and death.

"Simon Peter, who carried a sword, drew it and wounded the high priest's servant, cutting off his right ear. The servant's name was Malchus. Jesus said to Peter, 'Put your sword back in its scabbard; am I not to drink the cup that the Father has given me?'" (Jn. 18:10-11). The cup which had been promised in the Garden of Eden was now to be drunk in the Garden of Gethsemane. Jesus makes this point clear as he checks Peter's militant reaction. "Put your sword back, for all who draw the sword will die by the sword. Or do you think that I cannot appeal to my Father who would promptly send more than twelve legions of angels to my defense? But then, how would the scriptures be fulfilled that say this is the way it must be?" (Mt. 26:52-54). To understand Jesus' sense of mission, we must keep Genesis 3:14-15 in mind. Things are happening according to the divine plan which was revealed to our forebears in Eden. The struggle is not of human making or design.

"Then Jesus spoke to the chief priests and captains of the Temple guard and elders who had come for him. 'Am I a brigand that you had to set out with swords and clubs? When I was among you in the Temple day after day you never moved to lay hands on me. But this is your hour; this is the reign of darkness'" (Lk. 22:52-53). Jesus attempts to open the eyes of the leaders to the larger picture, but they refuse to see. The enlightened teachers are ensnared by the Prince of Darkness and thus become partners in a plot which is much larger than their own. Satan, surrounded by his minions, faces Jesus, who is standing alone and defenseless.

"The cohort and its captain with the Jewish guards seized Jesus and bound him" (Jn. 18:12). The Lord who had called Lazarus back from Sheol, the dwelling of the dead, and ordered him to be set free from his bonds is now bound and taken prisoner. "Then all the disciples deserted him and ran away" (Mt. 26:56). The first encounter with the opponent ends with a rout of all Jesus' supporters. The scene is spoken of in the prophet Amos.

> See then how I am going to crush you into the ground as the threshing sledge crushes when clogged by straw; flight will not save even the swift, the strong man will find his strength useless, the mighty man will be powerless to save himself. The bowman will not stand his ground, the faster runner will not escape, the horseman will not save himself, the bravest will run away naked that day (Am. 2:13-16).

Earlier, we heard the disciples claiming to have left all things to follow Jesus. On this night, Jesus is left alone. Mark tells us that one of the disciples left everything to get away from the Master. "A young man who followed him had nothing on but a linen cloth. They caught hold of him, but he left the cloth in their hands and ran away naked" (Mk. 14:51-52).

Just as David had faced Goliath alone and undefended, Jesus would undergo his ordeal with no one to defend him or plead his cause. It almost seems that Peter hoped to offer the Lord moral support. "Peter had followed him at a distance, right into the high priest's palace and was sitting with the attendants warming himself at the fire" (Mk. 14:54). We see this attitude of loving interest in Peter throughout the ministry of Jesus. Peter always felt the need to be near the Master, until things became uncomfortable, or something went wrong. "It was Peter who answered, 'Lord,' he said 'if it is you, tell me to come to you across the water.' 'Come' said Jesus. Then Peter got out of the boat and started walking towards Jesus across the water, but as soon as he felt the force of the wind, he took fright and began to sink" (Mt. 14:28-30). Finding himself in an awkward situation, fear overcomes him and Peter begins to sink.

We must remember, on the other hand, that the rest of the disciples never even left the boat. Likewise, it was Peter who followed Jesus into the courtyard, not the other disciples. "As Simon Peter stood there warming himself, someone said to him, 'Aren't you another of his disciples?' He denied it saying, 'I am not.' One of the high priest's servants, a relative of the man whose ear Peter had cut off said, 'Didn't I see you in the garden with him?' Again Peter denied it; and at once a cock crew" (Jn. 18:25-27). As Peter was sinking beneath the waves, Jesus reached out his hand and held him up until they returned to the boat. This night in the courtyard, Jesus will look at Peter, but Peter will find no peace or comfort, only fear and guilt. "Jesus turned and looked straight at Peter, and Peter remembered what the Lord had said to him, 'Before the cock crows today, you will have disowned me three times.' And he went outside and wept bitterly" (Lk. 22:61-62). Filled with fear and remorse, there is only one thing left for Peter to do: run.

God's champion, our *goel*, stands alone. While Caiaphas con-
venes the court, The Lord of Life and the Prince of Darkness
stand facing each other, waiting for the contest to begin.
Beneath the tension which fills the high priest's court one can
almost hear the cynical gloat, "At long last, I've got you!"

Eight

The Trial

Confused Justice and the Divine Plan

"The men who had arrested Jesus led him off to Caiaphas the high priest, where the scribes and the elders were assembled" (Mt. 26:57). The circumstances of Jesus' arrest and trial have attracted the interest of countless students of law and theology. The question which has kept so many occupied is why, exactly, Jesus was condemned to death. For generations, lawyers and theologians have attempted to unravel the legal, political, and religious intricacies of what has to be the most celebrated case of capital punishment. If we are accurately to answer the question, we must remember the "proto-gospel," Genesis 3:14. "When the Advocate comes, he will show the world how wrong it was, about sin, and about who was in the right and about judgment: about sin: proved by their refusal to believe in me; about who was in the right: proved by my going to the Father and your seeing me no more; about judgment: proved by the prince of this world being already condemned" (Jn. 16:8-11).

When Jesus stood before the Jewish court, they did not know his true identity, neither did they know their role in this great drama. Being faceless and nameless, they were unable to embrace the Truth, or put it into words. In one of his novels, C. S. Lewis makes this observation.

> When the time comes to you at which you will be forced at last to utter the speech which has been at the

> center of your soul for years, which you have, all that
> time, idiot-like, been saying over and over, you'll not
> talk about joy of words. I saw well why the gods do not
> speak to us openly, nor let us answer. Till that word can
> be dug out of us, why should they hear the babble that
> we think we mean? How can they meet us face to face
> till we have faces? *(Till We Have Faces).*

Jesus, the Truth of the Father, the Word made flesh, came to his own people, but they had clung to another image of the truth and would not open to him. Now the trial would proceed and judgement would verify the Truth.

"Now sentence is being passed on this world; now the prince of this world is to be overthrown. And when I am lifted up from the earth, I shall draw all men to myself" (Jn. 12:31-32). Satan will be crushed in the conflict. Through the victory of Christ, all of humanity will be brought to the fullness of truth and life. God's love is everlasting. The promise spoken to Adam and Eve in the garden is fulfilled in the person of Jesus. By meditating on the sacred passion of our Lord and Savior, Jesus Christ, we can grow in our appreciation of the meaning of redemption and salvation. Let us not cling to what we think to be true and reject the real truth in the process.

If we pare away all the non-essentials, the charges brought against Jesus were blasphemy and sedition. The religious leaders accused him of claiming to be the Messiah, the awaited savior of Israel; they also charged him with threatening to destroy the Temple. The gospels recount many incidents which make clear that Jesus did, in fact, have enemies among the leading classes of the Jews. He had criticized the Pharisees for their religiosity and went so far as to call them hypocrites. He argued with the Sadducees over points of theology and even espoused unconventional interpretations of the Law and Prophets. Jesus' demonstration in the Temple was perceived as a rejection of the Temple cult, an affront which the priests could not tolerate. They thought that there was no other choice but to take swift and decisive action against Jesus.

> Then the chief priests and Pharisees called a meeting.
> "Here is this man working all these signs" they said

"and what action are we taking? If we let him go on in this way everybody will believe in him, and the Romans will come and destroy the Holy Place and our nation." One of them, Caiaphas, the high priest that year, said, "You don't seem to have grasped the situation at all; you fail to see that it is better for one man to die for the people than for the whole nation to be destroyed" (Jn. 11:47-50).

The high priests had been trying to maintain an uneasy peace with the Romans. Their success at walking on the edge is seen in the fact that the Temple cult was tolerated by the emperor. When Jesus brought the Temple cult into question, he was upsetting the rapprochement which had been painstakingly achieved.

Judaism seems to have had the ability to allow for a wide range of theological difference. The Acts of the Apostles recounted one such debate.

Now Paul was well aware that one section was made up of Sadducees and the other Pharisees, so he called out in the Sanhedrin, "Brothers, I am a Pharisee and the son of Pharisees. It is for our hope in the resurrection of the dead that I am on trial." As soon as he said this a dispute broke out between the Pharisees and Sadducees, and the assembly was split between the two parties. For the Sadducees say there is neither resurrection, nor angel, nor spirit, while the Pharisees accept all three (Acts 23:6-8).

Theology could spark heated debates, so much so that the Sanhedrin could be easily divided. It would be impossible to get sufficient theological agreement in that assembly to account for Jesus' condemnation.

As is the case today, there seem to have been various degrees of observance among the Jews of Jesus' day. The interpretation of the Law would vary from casual to strict. Because of the existence of the diaspora in many lands, Judaism had become a cosmopolitan religion. Various groups would argue about the different points of observance but could never seem to agree upon any specific hard and fast rulings. Jesus was seen as just another voice in the discussion. "Then addressing the people and his disciples Jesus said, 'The scribes and the Pharisees occupy the chair of Moses. You must do what they tell you and listen to what they say; but do not be guided by what they do: since they do not practice what they preach. They tie up heavy burdens and lay them on men's shoulders, but will they lift a finger to move them? Not they!'" (Mt. 23:1-4). Certainly, such comments were taken to be offensive, but all people in public positions are targets of criticism. The fact that Jesus questioned the lifestyles of the scribes and Pharisees cannot be grounds for his condemnation. Jesus' own style of living was the subject of such criticism. "John the Baptist comes, not eating bread, not drinking wine, and you say, 'He is possessed.' The Son of Man comes, eating and drinking, and you say, 'Look! A glutton and a drunkard, a friend of tax collectors and sinners.' Yet Wisdom has been proved right by all her children" (Lk. 7:33-35). Jesus was a public figure and all his actions would be subject to scrutiny; any hint of inconsistency would be brought to his attention. Again, this may be matter for an interesting discussion or even a heated debate, but not grounds for crucifixion.

The reaction of the priests and scribes to Jesus' demonstration at the Temple does have a precedent in the life of the prophet Jeremiah.

> This word was addressed to Jeremiah by Yahweh. "Yahweh says this: If you will not listen to me by following my Law which I put before you, by paying attention to the words of my servants the prophets whom I send so persistently to you, without you ever listening to them, I will treat this Temple as I treated Shiloh, and make this city a curse for all the nations of the earth." The priests and prophets and all the people heard Jeremiah say these words in the Temple of Yahweh. When Jeremiah had finished saying everything that Yahweh has ordered him to say to all the people, the priests and prophets seized hold of him and said, "You shall die!" (Jer. 26:4-9).

The destruction of the Temple would signal the end of the

Jewish cult as it was known at that time. If the cult, as sym-
bolized by the Temple, were ended, the People of God would
no longer have a homeland. Just the thought of such destruction would send shudders of terror through any Jew. The more
militant would go to any extreme to stave off such an event. To
allow Jesus to continue to speak in such a vein would only
serve to inflame the zealots, bringing down the wrath of
Rome. Not to silence Jesus quickly and effectively would be
irresponsible on the part of the Sanhedrin.

> The chief priests and the whole Sanhedrin were looking
> for evidence against Jesus, however false, on which they
> might pass the death sentence. But they could not find
> any, though several lying witnesses came forward.
> Eventually two stepped forward and made a statement,
> "This man said: I have power to destroy the Temple of
> God and in three days build it up." The high priest then
> stood up and said to him, "Have you no answer at that?
> What is this evidence these men are bringing against
> you?" But Jesus was silent (Mt. 26:59-63).

Jesus is not there to argue with the chief priests; nor is he
there to debate with members of the Sanhedrin. His opponent
is Satan, and he will not allow himself to lose sight of this fact.

Many people saw what Jesus did that day in the Temple;
they also heard what he said. No one was willing to admit to
the truth of what could very easily happen if the kingdom of
God were truly in their midst. Throughout his ministry, Jesus
had done and said things which had been thought to be the
proper work or words of God alone. Jesus understood himself
to have a unique relationship with God, whom he publicly
addressed as "Father." How could the only God have a son?
Jesus was bringing into question the very cornerstone of
Jewish faith: "Hear O Israel, the Lord your God is God alone;
the Lord is One."

Israel was God's special people: Their identity was found
in their submission to the Law, in living on the land which God
had promised their forebears, in ordering their social and
political lives according to Moses and the Prophets, and in
desiring to experience the *Shekhenah* of God's presence in their

time. It was spiritual experience rather than ethnic roots which determined their national characteristics; Israel was a chosen people by virtue of the covenant which God himself had established with them through their ancestors. The one person who held this people together was the high priest, whom the common people believed to be the very incarnation of the Law. Anyone who represented a threat must be removed.

> Athaliah, on hearing the shouts of the people rushing to the king and acclaiming him, made for the Temple of Yahweh where the people were. When she saw the king standing there at the entrance beside the pillar, with the captains and trumpeters at the king's side, and all the country people rejoicing and sounding trumpets, and the cantors with their musical instruments leading the hymns, Athaliah tore her garments and shouted, "Treason, treason!" Then Jehoiada the priest called out the military officers. "Take her outside the precincts," he ordered, "and put anyone to the sword who follows her." For the priest had said, "You must not put her to death in the Temple of Yahweh." They seized her, and when she had reached the palace at the entry to the Gate of the Horses, they put her to death there (2 Chr. 23:12-15).

Acting on orders from the high priest, the Temple guard removed Athaliah from the Temple area and killed her. The high priest had the power over life and death and often played an important role in the history of the people. Caiaphas will wield a similar influence before the Sanhedrin. "And the high priest said to him, 'I put you on oath by the Living God to tell us if you are the Christ, the Son of God'" (Mt. 26:63). We can imagine Caiaphas seated upon his priestly throne, looking down at the prisoner and waiting for the reply. "Jesus said 'I am, and you will see the Son of Man seated at the right hand of the Power and coming with the clouds of heaven'" (Mk. 14:62).

Jesus had answered, using the vocabulary of Daniel's apocalyptic vision.

> I gazed into the visions of the night. And I saw, coming

on the clouds of heaven, one like a son of man. He came
to the one of great age and was led into his presence.
On him was conferred sovereignty, glory and kingship,
and men of all peoples, nations and languages became
his servants. His sovereignty is an eternal sovereignty
which shall never pass away, nor will his empire ever
be destroyed (Dn. 7:14).

In his demonstration at the Temple, Jesus spoke of the end
of the cult, the destruction of the Temple and the coming of the
heavenly city. This night, he identified himself as the One who
is to sit upon the heavenly throne. This was much more than
the high priest could bear. "At this, the high priest tore his
clothes and said, 'He has blasphemed. What need of witnesses have we now? There! You have heard the blasphemy. What
is your opinion?'" (Mt. 26:65-66).

The situation is very tense. Jesus is considered to be a holy
man by many of the people, yet he is espousing a doctrine
which would inflame the zealots to rise up against Rome.
Jesus' reply evokes a reaction from Caiaphas, who in turn asks
the council to render a judgment. "'We have a Law,' the Jews
said 'and according to that Law he ought to die, because he has
claimed to be the Son of God'" (Jn. 19:7). Jesus was captured
under the cover of night, but because of his notoriety, he could
not be put away secretly. The Temple which had been cleansed
by the Son of Man would not be desecrated by his blood. Jesus
would have to be ushered outside the gates. The Truth was
there, standing in their midst, but because he did not conform
with their interpretation of truth, they would not let him into
their lives. Rather, they would remove his name from the Book
of the Living, turning him over to the infidels who would com-
mend him to the dark recesses of Sheol.

Jesus knew what he was up against; he knew his real
adversary well. "He was a murderer from the start; he was
never grounded in the truth; there was no truth in him at all"
(Jn. 8:44). Satan, also known as the Accuser, was not one to
grant life; rather, he was known to repay those who served
him with death. Satan treats his pawns as swine or cannon
fodder. "Now there was there on the mountainside a great

herd of pigs feeding, and the unclean spirits begged him, 'Send us to the pigs, let us go into them!' So he gave them leave. With that, the unclean spirits came out and went into the pigs, and the herd of about two thousand pigs charged down the cliff into the lake, and there they were drowned" (Mk. 5:11-13). As Satan disposed of the pigs, so would he rid himself of Judas.

"When he found that Jesus had been condemned, Judas his betrayer was filled with remorse and took the thirty silver pieces back to the chief priests and elders. 'I have sinned;' he said 'I have betrayed innocent blood.' 'What is that to us?' they replied 'That is your concern.' And flinging down the silver pieces in the sanctuary he made off, and went and hanged himself" (Mt. 27:3-5). Judas' wage for playing his part was not the pouch of silver, but death at his own hand. Luke paints a graphic picture of Judas' death. "As you know, he bought a field with the money he was paid for his crime. He fell head-long and burst open, and all his entrails poured out" (Acts 1:18). In the beginning, God formed Adam out of the dust of the earth and breathed life into his body. In contrast, Satan dashes Judas' body against the ground and tears his life away from him.

Judas' desperate act of suicide stands in opposition to Jesus' faithful resignation to the Father's will throughout his passion. "The Father loves me, because I lay down my life in order to take it up again. No one takes it from me; I lay it down of my own free will, and as it is in my power to lay it down, so it is in my power to take it up again; and this is the command I have been given by my Father" (Jn. 10:17-18). No hapless victim of human plotting, Jesus is our *goel*, God's champion, who knowingly walks onto the field of combat to face Satan in the battle foretold in Genesis 3:14-15.

Nine

The Roman Trial

The Rulers of the World
Speak for the Prince of Darkness,
Jesus Is Rejected by the Human Race

"First thing in the morning, the chief priests together with the elders and scribes, in short the whole Sanhedrin, had their plan ready" (Mk. 15:1). As the King of the Jews, Jesus stands in the shadow of Moses. Now he will be taken to the court of the new Pharaoh, Pilate, with the task of leading his people out of the land of bondage. "The whole assembly rose, and they brought Jesus before Pilate" (Lk. 27:1). "They did not go into the Praetorium themselves or they would be defiled and unable to eat the Passover. So Pilate came outside to them" (Jn. 18:28-29). Jesus goes to his Passover as his people are celebrating theirs.

As his predecessor, Jehoiada, Caiaphas has his victim escorted away from the Temple grounds. Remember, Athaliah was led outside the gate and there she met her fate. So, too, with Jesus: the Temple will not be desecrated by the spilling of his blood, nor will the people who have come to Jerusalem to celebrate the Passover be rendered unclean by entering the gentile's residence. They did not realize, of course, that they had already been contaminated by the spirit of darkness and deceit. "Now I know, brothers, that neither you nor your leaders had any idea what you were really doing; this was the way God carried out what he had foretold, when he said through all his prophets that his Christ would suffer" (Acts 3:17-18).

For many historians, Jesus' conduct during the trial has proven a mystery. His apparent indifference to the charges brought against him has triggered many debates. There is an exchange between Jesus and Pilate in the Gospel of John which may serve as a suitable backdrop for our purposes. "Jesus said, 'I was born for this, I came into the world for this: to bear witness to the truth; and all who are on the side of truth listen to my voice.' 'Truth? What is that?' said Pilate" (Jn. 18:37-38). Jesus is consistently portrayed in Luke's gospel as being "on the road to Jerusalem." Everything that Jesus did throughout the ministry was geared toward the fulfillment of the Father's will and loving plan for universal salvation. Realizing that his time had come, Jesus stands before Pilate; his attitude is one of resolution, not indifference.

Earlier, we saw how Jesus told Peter to put his sword back into its scabbard. He was not going to meet force with force. Indeed, it has been suggested that while Satan was surrounded by his minions, Jesus stood in their midst alone and unarmed. Even when Jesus was the object of a violent assault, he did not respond in kind. However, he does ask his assailant to explain the reason for his action. "Jesus replied, 'If there is something wrong in what I said, point it out; but if there is no offense in it, why do you strike me?'" (Jn. 18:23). Jesus is fully aware of his reason for being; he remains true to his vision, no matter what the consequences for himself. "Then they spat in his face and hit him with their fists; others said as they struck him, 'Play the prophet, Christ! Who hit you then?'" (Mt. 26:67-68).

Mocked and treated as a fool, Jesus remains silent. This meekness and silence does not come from weakness of character or brokenness of will. In the face of utter failure, Jesus clings to his mission and does not alter his course. "Let us test him with cruelty and with torture, and thus explore this gentleness of his and put his endurance to the proof" (Wis. 2:19). It is for this reason that the early church began to understand Jesus in terms of the Suffering Servant of Isaiah. "Harshly dealt with, he bore it humbly, he never opened his mouth" (Is. 53:7).

It is dangerous to use political terms from one era and apply them to another. However, the vocabulary of nonviolent resistance used by Martin L. King and Gandhi before him seems to apply to the situation Jesus found himself in during his trial.

> At the center of nonviolence stands the principle of love. In struggling for human dignity the oppressed people of the world must not allow themselves to become bitter or indulge in hate campaigns. To retaliate with hate and bitterness would do nothing but intensify the hate in the world. Along the way of life, someone must have sense enough and morality enough to cut off the chain of hate. . . . Finally, the method of nonviolence is based on the conviction that the universe in on the side of justice. It is this deep faith in the future that causes the nonviolent resister to accept suffering without retaliation. He knows that in his struggle for justice he has cosmic companionship ("Nonviolence and Racial Justice").

Jesus is truth incarnate. Because he was faithful to the will of his Father, the truth of the actions taken against his person would come to light.

Having moved out of the Temple and the court of the high priest, we are introduced to yet another antagonist, Pontius Pilate. In each of the gospel accounts, the apparently indecisive and vacillating Roman procurator declares Jesus to be innocent of any capitol crime at one moment; at the next moment, he bows to the demands of the crowd and sentences Jesus to death. Over the years, authors have painted various portraits of Pilate, the man. Some have suggested that there may have been political reasons for Pilate's behavior. He had been reprimanded by the emperor Tiberius on two previous occasions. He could not afford another incident or he would be placed under imperial censure. It was necessary that he prevent any outbreak of anti-Roman sentiments, especially now during the Passover, when the city was overcrowded with pious pilgrims. It might be good to recall the words of Satan to Jesus while tempting him, "I will give you all this power and the glory of these kingdoms, for it has been committed to me and I give it to anyone I choose" (Lk. 4:6).

"Pilate came outside to them and said, 'What charge do you bring against this man?' They replied, 'If he were not a criminal, we should not be handing him over to you'" (Jn. 18:29-30). Jesus' crime is that he stood up against the "ruler of this world." The conflict is between the Lord of Life and the Prince of Darkness, no one else. "They began their accusations by saying, 'We found this man inciting our people to revolt, opposing payment of tribute to Caesar, and claiming to be the Christ, a king.' Pilate put to him this question, 'Are you the King of the Jews?' 'It is you who say it,' Jesus replied. Pilate asked if the man were a Galilean; and finding that he came under Herod's jurisdiction he passed him over to Herod who was in Jerusalem at that time" (Lk. 23:6-7). As King of the Jews, Jesus is no threat to the Jewish religion; rather, he would prove an enemy to the authority of Rome. Pilate is not concerned about the life of this itinerant preacher as much as he is about his own status in the eyes of the emperor. Faced with this apparent challenge by the high priests, Pilate is looking for a way to bring about a rapprochement with his adversaries. Pilate's action was a diplomatic move, aimed at improving relations with Herod by recognizing his jurisdiction in Galilean affairs.

The gospels recount the fact that Herod had ordered the execution of John the Baptizer. "Meanwhile Herod the tetrarch had heard about all that was going on; and he was puzzled, because some people were saying that John has risen from the dead, others that Elijah had reappeared, still others that one of the ancient prophets had come back to life. But Herod said, 'John? I beheaded him. So who is this I hear such reports about?' And he was anxious to see him" (Lk. 9:7-9). Pilate's gesture would serve to satisfy Herod's curiosity. Such a meeting would allow the reigning monarch to determine if the prophet from Nazareth posed any real threat to his throne, or to the peace of Israel.

"Herod was delighted to see Jesus; he had heard about him and had been wanting for a long time to set eyes on him; moreover, he was hoping to see some miracle worked by him. So he questioned him at some length; but without getting any reply.

. . . Then Herod, together with his guards, treated him with contempt and made fun of him; he put a rich cloak on him and sent him back to Pilate" (Lk. 23:8-9, 11). The conflict is not between Jesus and the holy people Israel. Rather, the Son of the Woman is to confront the lord of this world, personified in Pilate. Thus, Herod sends the prisoner back to the praetorium.

Unlike John, Jesus did not criticize Herod's marital status. Neither does Jesus join ranks with the zealots who strongly oppose Herod's rule, because they consider him to be a puppet of Rome. Earlier, Herod the Great, had felt threatened at the news of the birth of Son of David in Bethlehem, and ordered the slaughter of the innocent children at the breast. Standing before the survivor of that infanticide, Herod now sees only a foolish human, fit for nothing but mockery and derision. Clearly, this Jesus was no threat to his throne, not anything like John whom he had beheaded. The gospels tell us that Pilate's shrewd strategy had worked and an unpleasant incident had been averted. "Though Herod and Pilate had been enemies before, they were reconciled that same day" (Lk. 23:12). Having pacified Herod, Pilate was free to hear the case and dispose of Jesus in any fashion he saw fit. However, to crucify this man, Pilate needed a crime. Herod had judged Jesus to be little more than a fool to be ridiculed; and Jewish beliefs were of no concern to Rome. What crime had he committed?

As Jesus returns to Pilate's court, the true antagonist begins to manipulate the crowd. A description of the interplay between Satan and the power of Rome is given in the Book of Revelation. "I was standing on the seashore. Then I saw a beast emerge from the sea: it had seven heads and ten horns, with a coronet on each of its ten horns, and its heads were marked with blasphemous titles. I saw that the beast was like a leopard, with paws like a bear and a mouth like a lion; the dragon had handed over to it his own power and his throne and his worldwide authority" (Rv. 12:18–13:2). Satan, through his agent, Pilate, is brought face-to-face with the champion of God's chosen people. The contest is begun.

The atmosphere is totally changed. No longer do the high priests implore God to make manifest his eternal justice; no longer do the pilgrims flock to the Temple precincts to offer the pleasant odor of burnt sacrifice; now they all come into territory not their own and fill the air with shouts of rejection and cries of condemnation. A description of the din is found in the *Screwtape Letters*, by C. S. Lewis, spoken from among the ranks of Satan's forces.

> Music and silence—how I detest them both! How thankful we should be that ever since our Father entered Hell—though longer ago than humans, reckoning in light years, could express—no square inch of infernal space and no moment of infernal time has been surrendered to either of these abominable forces, but all has been occupied by noise. Noise, the grand dynamism, the audible expression of all that is exultant, ruthless, and virile. Noise which alone defends us from silly qualms, despairing scruples, and impossible desires. We will make the whole universe a noise in the end. We have already made great strides in this direction as regards the earth. The melodies and silences of heaven will be shouted down in the end. But I admit we are not yet loud enough, or anything like it (*Screwtape Letters*).

While Jesus remains silent, those standing around him shout, refusing to hear the Word of Truth. They are wrapped in an infernal din. "Pilate was anxious to set Jesus free and addressed them again, but they shouted back, 'Crucify him! Crucify him!' And for the third time he spoke to them, 'Why? What harm has he done? I have found no case against him that deserves death, so I shall have him punished and then let him go.' But they kept on shouting at the top of their voices, demanding that he should be crucified. And their shouts were growing louder" (Lk. 23:20-23). The shouts provide Satan's needed noise, a noise intended to shout down heaven itself. "They all said, 'Let him be crucified!' 'Why?' he asked. 'What harm has he done?' But they shouted all the louder, 'Let him be crucified!' Then Pilate saw that he was making no impression, that in fact a riot was imminent. So he took some water, washed his hands in front of the crowd and said, 'I am innocent of this man's blood. It is your concern'" (Mt. 27:23-25). If Pilate had any qualms about sending Jesus to the cross, the noise of the crowd deafened him to his scruples. The shouting continued and the ears of those who were crying for Jesus' death heard nothing. The voices blended into one continuous roar, giving expression to emotions which were more ruthless and violent. "They shouted all the louder, 'Crucify him!' So Pilate, anxious to placate the crowd, released Barabbas for them and having ordered Jesus to be scourged, handed him over to be crucified" (Mk. 15:14-15).

As the noise becomes more intense, and the shouts grow in volume, hate becomes almost tangible. Pilate serves as the grand marshal of the duel. The noise of hell attempts to drown out the silence of the kingdom of God, yet, in the midst of all this display stands the Holy One of Israel. Jesus stands before his foe, mindful of the Father's love for him. "The Father loves me, because I lay down my life in order to take it up again. No one takes it from me; I lay it down of my own free will, and as it is in my power to lay it down, so it is in my power to take it up again; and this is the command I have been given by my Father" (Jn. 10:17-18).

Ten

The Scourging at the Pillar

The Victim Is Prepared,
the King Is Anointed and Crowned

"The governor's soldiers took Jesus with them into the Praetorium and collected the whole cohort around him. Then they stripped him" (Mt. 27:27-28). This scourging, this brutal beating, was an integral part of the process of crucifixion. Although the severity of the scourging is not discussed in the gospel accounts, it is implied in the First Letter of Peter: "He was bearing our faults in his own body on the cross, so that we might die to our faults and live for holiness; through his wounds you have been healed" (1 Pt. 2:24). Commentaries on this passage state that the words used indicate that the scourging Jesus received was particularly severe. The Prince of Peace is brutalized by the soldiers of Rome, the masters of the world.

One can only wonder why Jesus was the target of such harsh treatment. We do not read in any of the accounts that Jesus has offered his captors any resistance. In the garden, when he is betrayed by Judas, he stays the hand of Peter and surrenders himself into the hands of Temple police. Throughout the process of the hearing before Caiaphas and the trial before Pilate, he is passive, allowing himself to become the brunt of their mockery. He lived according to his own teaching: "Love your enemies, do good to those who hate you, bless those who curse you, pray for those who treat you badly. To the man who slaps you on one cheek, present the other cheek too; to the man who takes your cloak from you, do not refuse your tunic. Give to everyone who asks you, and do not ask for your property back from the man who robs you" (Lk. 6:27-30).

Torture and public execution have two principal purposes: to dehumanize and demoralize the victim and also to terrorize the local populace. Once punished, the individual would be placed on public display as a warning to others. The louder the screams of pain or the pleading for mercy, the more bloody and gruesome the torture, the better the object lesson. A silent or submissive victim would not serve the dual intent of the executioner. The Austrian writer, Franz Werfel describes such a scene in one of his novels.

> The saptiehs pushed Stephan out of the cart. The mudir ordered him to strip; there might be some writing hidden on his naked body. Stephan did it so quietly and indifferently that the crowd mistook his peace for sullenness; it enraged the onlookers. Even before he was quite naked, someone had punched the back of his head. . . . The first knife was thrust into Stephan's back. . . . His body was covered with forty wounds, knife and bayonet thrusts in the back, a broken neck and a slit throat (*The Forty Days of Musa Dagh*).

If they could not make the victim squirm and beg for mercy, they would slowly and methodically murder him.

The victim would be tortured to make sure that he knew that he was nothing but a plaything for his tormentors and to break his will. The more willful the victim, the greater the pain inflicted to guarantee the first objective. The scriptures recount such an increase of intensity of torture. "The king fell into a rage and treated the seventh son more cruelly than the others, for he was himself smarting from the young man's scorn. And so the last brother met his end undefiled and with perfect trust in the Lord" (2 Mc. 7:39-40).

Jesus follows the soldiers into the compound neither begging for mercy nor pleading for his life. He has come to do the Father's will, to which he has made total submission. Movies often portray the soldiers ripping Jesus' clothes off his back, but since the condemned man's clothing would also serve as the executioner's pay, there is good reason to believe the soldiers would not damage their property. John's account of the crucifixion tells us that the guards did not wish to tear Jesus' garment since it was seamless (cf. Jn. 19:23-24). It seems more likely that someone threw a basket to Jesus and ordered him to strip, placing all his belongings in the basket. If Werfel's description is valid, the guard probably mocked the prisoner as he removed his clothes. In Eden, God covers the shameful nakedness of sinful Adam and Eve. In the praetorium, the sinless Son of God stands naked and without shame before the ridicule of the Roman cohort.

Perhaps the soldiers are taken by surprise at Jesus' composure and demeanor as he removed his clothing. Despite their crude jokes and taunts, he never loses sight of his goal: to be obedient to the Father's will. He stands before them, a man with a mission to fulfill, and he will not be intimidated. Naked and unashamed, he hands the basket over to the guard who points to the pillar. With the same determination which brought him to Jerusalem, he walks to the place of torture and stretches out his hands for the soldiers to tie them in place for the ordeal. "For my part, I made no resistance, neither did I turn away. I offered my back to those who struck me" (Is. 50:5). Naked and defenseless, Jesus becomes the plaything of the Romans and the brunt of their bigotry, hatred, and cynicism. Certainly, they are not ignorant of the identity of their "honored" guest. They may have heard reports of his miracles or had heard him preaching to the crowds. They might have known the centurion whose servant was cured. All this was history. Now, however, the preacher and wonder worker is to be scourged and the soldiers were well trained in the art of torture. "With these words Eleazar went straight to the block. His escorts, so recently well disposed towards him, turned against him" (2 Mc. 6:29).

Scourging was the preliminary stage to every Roman execution. The usual instrument of torture was a short whip made of braided leather thongs into which small iron balls or pieces of sheep bone were tied at intervals. The victim would be fastened to a pillar and beaten from behind. Usually two soldiers would be used to inflict the punishment; if only one was available, he would alternate positions to guarantee the proper distribution of lashes. Seeing as an entire cohort was gathered around Jesus, it is safe to surmise that at least two people wielded the flagella. Unlike Jewish penal code, the Romans did not limit the number of strokes. The severity of the scourging depended on the disposition of the soldiers and the constitution of the victim: the condemned man was to die on the cross and not at the pillar. The flogging was geared to insure the maximum experience of pain throughout the dying process and would be stopped before the prisoner collapsed.

In his meekness, Jesus was the object of insult and scorn as he stood before the Temple guards. "Some of them started spitting at him and, blindfolding him, began hitting him with their fists and shouting, 'Play the prophet!' And the attendants rained blows on him" (Mk. 14:65). If the Temple guard playfully started beating him after the meeting of the Sanhedrin, one could easily imagine what the Roman soldiers would do to him. When the high priest brought the prisoner to Pilate, he did not condemn him for being a preacher or for working miracles. Rather, he told him, "He has claimed to be the Son of God" (Jn. 19:7). It is one thing to ridicule a prophet or visionary; but it is quite another to break the strength of the "Son of God." What the Jewish guard had begun with crude mockery, the Romans would finish with practiced brutality and deadly seriousness.

In a book dealing with the history of Russia, Robert K. Massie describes the use of a single thonged whip, called a knout.

> A blow from the knout tore skin from the bare back of a victim and, when the lash fell repeatedly in the same place, could bite through to the bone. . . . Applying the knout was skilled work. The wielder first making a step back and giving a spring forward at every stroke which is laid with such force that the blood flies at every stroke and leaves a weal behind as thick as a man's finger. The knout masters are so exact in their work that they rarely

strike two strokes in the same place, but laid them on the whole length and breadth of a man's back, by the side of each other with great dexterity from the top of a man's shoulders downward *(Peter the Great)*.

If this much damage can be done to a human being with a single flat leather strap, what must have been the effect of the Roman flagellum?

Flogging was intended to maim and disfigure the victim. The intensity of each blow would send shocks of pain throughout the victim's entire frame, sapping away all bodily strength. The torture would continue until the victim would beg for mercy, having finally been broken as a person, having no will to resist any further. T. E. Lawrence (better known as Lawrence of Arabia) writes of a flogging he received when arrested in Deraa, Syria.

He saw me shivering, partly I think, with cold, and made the whip whistle over my ear, taunting me that with his tenth cut I would howl for mercy. . . . Then he began to lash me madly across and across with all his might, while I locked my teeth to endure this thing which lapped itself like flaming wire about my body. . . . To keep my mind in control I numbered the blows, but after twenty lost count, and could feel only the shape-less weight of pain, hot tearing claws, for which I had prepared, but a gradual cracking apart of my whole being by some too-great force whose waves rolled up my spine till they were pent within my brain, to clash terribly together. . . . My head would be pulled round to see how a hard white ridge, leaped over my skin at the instant of each stroke, with a bead of blood where two ridges crossed. As the punishment proceeded the whip fell more and more upon existing weals, biting blacker or more wet, till my flesh quivered with accu-mulated pain, and with terror of the next blow coming. They soon conquered my determination not to cry. . . . At last when I was completely broken they seemed satisfied. . . . Within me the core of life seemed to heave slowly up through the rending nerves *(Seven Pillars of Wisdom)*.

Lawrence's comments indicate that the repeated use of the lash added to the terror inflicted. The use of a multiple thonged whip would intensify the agony. The soldiers would strike Jesus' back with full force allowing the thongs to create their weals while the iron balls would cause deep contusions and the sharp edges of the bits of bone would cut through the fleshy tissue. With repeated strokes, the thongs would bite into the underlying skeletal muscles and tear out bleeding ribbons of flesh. It is possible that a number of soldiers may have vied for an opportunity to wield the whip and challenge each other to match force of impact, stroke for stroke. The combination of excruciating pain and excessive loss of blood would have put the victim into circulatory shock. From a medical point of view, Jesus' condition would have been serious, bordering on critical, at the end of the flogging.

Massie describes the mental state of a victim after being put under the knout. "First came examination under torture. On June 19, Alexis received twenty-five blows of the knout. No new confession was wrung from him by this pain, and on June 24 torture was applied again. With fifteen more strokes of the knout tearing the flesh off his back in bloody ribbons. In that abject state, he was ready to admit anything" (Peter the Great). In the cases of Lawrence of Arabia and Alexis, the beatings continued until the victim no longer had the strength to resist. Once every vestige of self-esteem and self-mastery was torn from the individual, the crack of the lash stopped. There seems to have been a certain proportion involved: the stronger the will of the victim to withstand the pain, the harder the strokes. Only when the victim was reduced to a limp mass of blood and torn flesh would the arm wielding the lash be stayed.

Finally, the centurion orders his men to stop. The slap of leather against flesh is no longer heard. Clinging to the last vestiges of consciousness, Jesus emits a groan as every nerve in his body throbs with pain. His frame quakes as a fever overtakes him. His knees buckle under the weight of his tormented body, and he hangs from the ropes which bind him to the pillar. "So disfigured did he look that he seemed no longer human" (Is. 52:14). Seeing the effects of their efforts, the soldiers may have complimented themselves on a "job well done." As the Temple guard had impaired the vision of a prophet; they had broken the strength of the Son of God.

The scourging done, the condemned man is untied from the pillar and allowed to sit for a while. Suddenly, one of the soldiers remembered that this man had been called "The King of the Jews." It just did not seem right that he sit there without proper regalia. Seeing as they had anointed him in blood and sweat, they proceed to drape a scarlet cloak over his quivering flesh and hold a mock coronation. "Having twisted some thorns into a crown they put it on his head, and they placed a reed in his right hand. To make fun of him, they knelt before him saying, 'Hail, King of the Jews!' and they spat on him and took the reed and struck him on the head with it" (Mt. 27:29-30). In humble submission, he accepts their mock homage, knowing that he is doing his Father's will.

There Jesus sits, exposed to our gaze. He is the object of hatred and the victim of human cruelty. In this weakened state, God's champion goes forth to engage his adversary, the Prince of Darkness, willingly accepting the blows so that we may win the glory. We must never forget that Jesus could have handled things differently, but that he freely chose not to. "Do you think that I cannot appeal to my Father who would promptly send more than twelve legions of angels to my defense?" (Mt. 26:53). Martin L. King offers these reflections.

> Somehow we must be able to stand up before our most bitter opponents and say: We shall match your capacity to inflict suffering by our capacity to endure suffering. We shall meet your physical force with soul force. Do to us what you will and we will still love you. We cannot in all good conscience obey your unjust laws and abide by the unjust system, because noncooperation with evil is as much a moral obligation as is cooperation with good, and so throw us in jail and we will still love you. Bomb our homes and threaten our children, and, as difficult as it is, we will still love you. Send your hooded perpetrators of violence into our communities at the midnight hour and drag us out on some wayside road and leave us half-dead as you beat

us, and we will still love you. Send your propaganda
agents around the country, and make it appear that we
are not fit, culturally and otherwise, for integration,
and we will still love you. But be assured that we'll
wear you down by our capacity to suffer, and one day
we will win our freedom. We'll not only win freedom
for ourselves; we will so appeal to your hearts and con-
science that we will win you in the process, and our victory will be a double victory *(A Testament of Hope)*.

Eleven

Via Crucis

From Faltering Limbs to Eagle's Wings

"Now as the time drew near for him to be taken up to heaven, he resolutely took the road for Jerusalem" (Lk. 9:51). During the mock coronation ceremony and while he received the "homage" of the soldiers, Jesus was able to regroup his energies for the next phase of his ordeal. Feeling strength returning to his limbs, he stands and turns his face towards Calvary.

"They then took charge of Jesus, and carrying his own cross he went out of the city to the place of the skull or, as it is called in Hebrew, Golgotha" (Jn. 19:17). The image of Jesus, crowned with thorns and carrying a cross brings to mind "the song of the vineyard" which was sung by the prophet Isaiah.

> Let me sing to my friend the song of his love for his vineyard. My friend had a vineyard on a fertile hillside. He dug the soil, cleared it of stones, and planted choice vines in it. In the middle he built a tower, he dug a press there too. He expected it to yield grapes, but sour grapes were all that it gave. . . . Yes, the vineyard of Yahweh Sabaoth is the House of Israel, and the men of Judah that chosen plant. He expected justice, but found bloodshed, integrity, but only a cry of distress (Is. 5:1-2, 7).

It was customary for the condemned man to carry his own cross to the crucifixion site. The total weight of the cross has been estimated at three hundred pounds, a burden which would tax even a robust youth. Thus it seems likely that only the crossbar, which only weighed between seventy-five and one hundred and twenty-five pounds, was actually carried by the victim. The beam would be placed across the nape of the neck and balanced on the shoulders. To help stabilize the load, it would be tied to his outstretched arms. With the weight of the crossbar so distributed and held in place, the victim could carry his burden with a minimum of difficulty. Every phase of the punishment was so measured as to weaken the criminal and intensify the pain, but not to kill him. The Romans made sure that the condemned man died on the cross and not on his way to it.

The procession to the crucifixion site was led by a military guard which was under the command of a centurion. A soldier went before the criminal carrying a sign, called a *titulus*, upon which was inscribed the man's name and the crime for which he was being punished. Once the sentence had been executed, the *titulus* was hung on the cross. This practice is noted in the passion accounts:

> Pilate wrote out a notice and had it fixed to the cross; it ran: "Jesus the Nazarene, King of the Jews." This notice was read by many of the Jews because the place where Jesus was crucified was not far from the city, and the writing was in Hebrew, Latin and Greek. So the Jewish chief priests said to Pilate, "You should not write 'King of the Jews,' but 'This man said: I am King of the Jews.'" Pilate answered, "What I have written, I have written" (Jn. 19:19-22).

The Lion of Judah is paraded before the people, covered with blood, cloaked in mock-regal splendor, and carrying the plank which will serve as his throne. The all-night ordeal of the trials, beginning with the Sanhedrin and ending with the judgment of Pilate, had made it impossible for Jesus to sleep or take any recuperative rest. Added to the physical exhaustion and the mental drain, the Temple guard had beaten and physically abused him. When the Romans had finished the flogging, Jesus did not have the strength to support his own body weight, let alone the added weight of the crossbeam. This picture can easily confirm the tradition of Jesus falling along the way to

Golgotha. Yet, we see Jesus pushing himself to reach his goal, the fulfillment of his Father's will that he contend with the Prince of Darkness and thus set the people free. "I have trodden the winepress alone. Of the men of my people not one was with me. In my anger I trod them down, trampled them in my wrath. Their juice spattered my garments, and all my clothes are stained. For in my heart was a day of vengeance, my year of redemption had come. I looked: there was no one to help; aghast: not one could I find to support me. My own arm then was my mainstay, my wrath my support" (Is. 63:3-5).

Moral fortitude and interior drive do not, however, compensate for physical exhaustion. The excruciating pain of the flogging and a general state of physical exhaustion leave him on the edge of consciousness. Dazed and feeble, his steps falter, his minimal level of strength ebbs and his stamina wanes. Shortly after beginning the final trek which will bring him to Calvary, Jesus stumbles and falls to the ground. The Son of God, who is the Creator and Master of the Universe, lies before mortal gaze, pinned under the wood which will soon hold him aloft. The God who set all the planets in motion is unable to move. St. Paul does not want us to miss the lesson of this sight.

> In your minds you must be the same as Christ Jesus: His state was divine, yet he did not cling to his equality with God but emptied himself to assume the condition of a slave, and became as men are; and being as all men are, he was humbler yet, even to accepting death, death on a cross. But God raised him high as gave him the name which is above all other names so that all beings in the heavens, on earth and in the underworld, should bend the knee at the name of Jesus and that every tongue should acclaim Jesus Christ as Lord, to the glory of God the Father (Phil. 2:5-11).

In Jesus, we see the champion of God and the mystery of spiritual warfare. Not only does he empty himself of the glory that is his as God, but he also lays down his human dignity for the sake of our salvation. In order to find the strength to overcome Satan, we must be brought to the ground of our human weakness.

The Romans had perfected the process of crucifixion so as to produce the maximum of pain for the victim. However, when they saw the motionless mass of bleeding human flesh pinned to the ground by the crossbar, they realized that they had not exercised prudential judgment while putting Jesus to the lash. Seeing that he was already moribund, they knew that they would have to act quickly or he would die before reaching Calvary. "As they were leading him away they seized on a man, Simon from Cyrene, who was coming in from the country and made him shoulder the cross behind Jesus" (Lk. 23:26). According to pious tradition, Simon was an unwilling helper. However, having taken up Christ's cross and followed him, he found his being was filled with the spirit of faith and love. By the time they reached the place of execution, the burden which he had first shouldered unwillingly and with distaste, he carried with joy. The moral of the story is encapsulated in the Rule of St. Benedict. "Do not be daunted immediately by fear and run away from the road that leads to salvation. It is bound to be narrow at the outset. But as we progress in this way of life and in faith, we shall run on the path of God's commandments, our hearts overflowing with the inexpressible delight of love" (*The Rule of St. Benedict*).

The devotion called the Stations of the Cross presents us with a diptych. On one side is the unwilling man Simon of Cyrene; on the other is the thoughtful and compassionate woman Veronica. Simon is drafted by the soldiers to help Jesus, Veronica pushes her way past the guard to comfort the Lord. Gently she wipes the blood and sweat from that tortured face. Motivated by love and compassion, she is blind to the possible abuse she might receive. Having heard the voice of the beloved, she is deaf to the shouts of the crowd. All she saw was a human being who was in need. The man whom she called "Master" was degraded to this humble state and was too weak to even wipe his own brow. She had listened and internalized the message of Jesus' preaching. She had put into practice the lessons which were read in the synagogue. "A faithful friend is a sure shelter, whoever finds one has found a rare treasure. A faithful friend is something beyond price, there is no measuring his worth. A faithful friend is the elixir of life, and those who fear the Lord will find one. Whoever fears the Lord makes true friends, for as a man is, so is his friend" (Sir. 6:14-17). Tradition has it that an imprint of Christ's features remained on the cloth after she wiped his face. In fact, the Savior seals with his own image every act of loving kindness which is performed in his name.

According to the Talmud, there was a group of women in Jerusalem who were in the practice of offering the condemned man a mildly drugged potion to serve as an anodyne for the pain. "They offered him wine mixed with myrrh, but he refused it" (Mk. 15:23). Jesus would not allow his pain to be mitigated. The first Adam had sought ways to avoid God's will for him; Jesus would embrace the Father's will with all its implications. God's champion, our *goel*, would enter the arena and face our infernal enemy enduring every pain and suffering that we are wont to avoid; in his endurance is our victory. We who seek to avoid and deny our human weakness stand before the Son of God who emptied himself of power and strength.

"Who could believe what we have heard, and to whom has the power of Yahweh been revealed? Like a sapling he grew up in front of us, like a root in arid ground, without beauty, without majesty, no looks to attract our eyes; a thing despised and rejected by men, a man of sorrows and familiar with suffering, a man to make people screen their faces; he was despised and we took no account of him" (Is. 53:1-3). The women had seen the effects of hatred and violence; they felt the anguish in their very beings. They had wanted to show Jesus some measure of compassion, and his rejection of this small gesture struck them to the quick. "But Jesus turned to them and said, 'Daughters of Jerusalem, do not weep for me; weep rather for yourselves and for your children. For the days will surely come when people will say, "Happy are those who are barren, the wombs that have never borne, the breasts that have never suckled!" Then they will begin to say to the mountains, "Fall on us!"; to the hills, "Cover us!" For if men use the green wood like this, what will happen when it is dry?'" (Lk. 23:28-31).

The feelings of the women, and of all who stood helplessly watching Jesus die, are captured in these lines from C. S. Lewis.

> And then one or other dies. And we think of this as love cut short; like a dance stopped in mid career or a flower with its head unluckily snapped off. . . . We are taken out of ourselves by the loved one while she is here. Then comes the tragic figure of the dance in which we must learn to be still taken out of ourselves though the bodily presence is withdrawn, to love the very Her, and not fall back to loving our past, or our memory, or our sorrow, or our relief from sorrow, or our own love (*A Grief Observed*).

Twelve

The Crucifixion

The Paschal Lamb Is Slain, Jesus Becomes Our Atonement

Kol Nidre

hymn for Yom Kippur

All personal vows we are likely to make, all personal oaths we are likely to take between this Yom Kippur and the next Yom Kippur, we publicly renounce. Let them all be relinquished and abandoned, null and void, neither firm nor established. Let our personal vows, pledges and oaths, be considered neither vows nor pledges nor oaths. May all the people of Israel be forgiven, including all the strangers who live in their midst, for all the people are in fault. O pardon the iniquities of this people, according to thy abundant kindness, even as thou hast forgiven this people ever since they left Egypt.

Crucifixion originated among the Persians who impaled the bodies of their victims on a stake. Alexander the Great brought the practice to Egypt and Carthage. The Romans learned of it from the Carthaginians. While the Romans were not the originators of crucifixion, they did perfect it as a form of torture. They employed it as a form of capital punishment, designed as a slow and extremely painful death. As such, it was considered the most disgraceful and cruel method of execution and was usually reserved for slaves, foreigners, revolutionaries, and the vilest of criminals. Roman law usually protected a Roman citizen from crucifixion, except in the case of desertion from the army. Seneca the Younger left us a letter in which he stated it would be preferable to commit suicide than undergo crucifixion.

> Can anyone be found who would prefer wasting away in pain, dying limb by limb, or letting out his life drop by drop rather than by expiring once for all? Can any man be found willing to be fastened to the accursed tree feverish and sickly, already deformed, swelling with ugly weals on shoulders and chest, and drawing in the breath of life amid long drawn out agony? He would have many excuses for dying, even before mounting the cross (letter 101).

While some of the details may be disputed, the fact that Jesus of Nazareth, a man in his late 20s or early 30s, was executed in Roman-occupied Palestine is one part of the passion narrative which is well corroborated by extra-biblical sources. The historian Tacitus, writing in the year 110 of the persecution of Christians under the Emperor Nero calls them "followers of Christ, whom the procurator Pontius Pilate had executed in the reign of Tiberius." While distorting his family origins, the Talmud records the fact that Jesus "was crucified on the eve of Passover because he seduced Israel, leading her astray."

Because it was a particularly gruesome form of punishment, crucifixion was used especially to make an example of prisoners whom the Romans considered insurgents. In 1968, archaeologists came upon some evidence which closely corroborated details recounted in the passion narratives. At an excavation site near Mount Scopus, a tomb was discovered which held the remains of a man who had been crucified some time before the destruction of the Temple. The most dramatic evidence that this man had been crucified was the nail which penetrated his heel bones. As the bones were taken out of the ossuary and put together, it was possible to tell how he died. The tibia had been brutally fractured into large, sharp splinters. Evidently, this fracture was produced by a single, sharp blow. When the arm bones were inspected, a small scratch was noted on the radius of the right forearm, just above the wrist.

Such a scratch could have been caused by the compression, friction, and gliding of an object such as a nail on the fresh bone.

The Roman cross was characterized by an upright post *(stipes)* and a horizontal crossbar *(patibulum)*, but it had many variations. Although archaeological and historical evidence strongly indicated that the low Tau cross was preferred by the Romans in Palestine at the time of Jesus, crucifixion practices did vary region to region. The Romans had a genius for refining this torture. To prolong the agony, a small seat, known as the *sedile*, was attached to the front of the cross, allowing the victim to support his body weight on more than just the nail which fastened his feet to the upright. The skeletal remains found at Mount Scopus would lead us to believe that the individual would have only rested one buttock on the *sedile*, his ankles being nailed so as to twist the hips to one side. Because the seat prevented the total collapse of the body, which would have caused the victim to hang at length from the nails in the wrists, the man could live on the cross for an extended period of time. Human genius, however, was not the only cause of pain and suffering. We often forget the fact that Palestine was hot and muggy, a seedbed for insects and vermin. Flies and other insects would light upon the open wounds. With hands nailed fast, the crucified individual could not swat these pests away from eyes, ears, or nose. After reading accounts of torture victims who were left exposed to the elements, it is not unrealistic to surmise that some birds of prey would likewise have lighted on the cross and picked at the lacerated flesh. In addition to these indignities, we have the problem of discharging human waste. Granted, our age may be more sensitive to some notions of decorum, but it is hard to imagine a form of torture which is more demeaning or dehumanizing than crucifixion.

"When they reached the place call The Skull, they crucified him there and the two criminals also, one on the right, the other on the left" (Lk. 23:33). The procession from the praetorium ended, the soldiers proceed to carry out the sentence in typical Roman fashion. With the practiced ease, they set up ladders, prepared hammers, nails, and ropes, and prepared the crossbeam. The King of the Jews no longer requires his regalia; the cloak is stripped from his tortured frame. The cloth which had clung to the bloody flesh reopens all the wounds left by the lash. A shock of indescribable pain shoots through his being and finally explodes in his head. Having refused the cup of compassion from the women, Jesus continues to drink deeply of the cup which his Father had willed for him. "And this is what he said, on coming into the world: You who wanted no sacrifice or oblation, prepared a body for me. You took no pleasure in holocausts or sacrifices for sin; then I said, just as I was commanded in the scroll of the book: God, here I am! I am coming to obey your will" (Heb. 10:5-7). With every wound, every spasm of pain, every wrenched muscle, every trickle of blood; with all the exhaustion of his being and weakness of his limbs, with every bruise and laceration sustained while put under the lash, Jesus stands prepared to do the Father's will.

Even before the wave of pain clears his head, he is thrown down to the ground and his arms are stretched to the ends of the crossbeam. Soldiers with hammers in hand quickly drive the spikes through the flesh, between the ulna and radius of the forearm, and finally lodge them deep in the wood. It only took a few heavy blows of the hammer to fix the victim's arms to the cross. The soldiers then lifted the beam, dragging Jesus to his feet; for a moment he hangs suspended from the nails in his wrists as the *patibulum* is fitted to the *stipes*. As he swings against the *sedile* with all his weight, a shock of pain would flash through every nerve in his back. With his hands fastened to the cross, he can do nothing but wait as the soldiers prepare to nail his feet in place.

His knees are bent and thrust to one side. A nail is driven through a small wooden plaque which is meant to keep the feet from sliding over the head of the nail. Then the feet were held in place, exposing the heel bone, through which the nail passed. Finally, the nail was pounded until it was lodged firmly in the wood. In order to allow the victim to raise himself up on the nail so as to allow his lungs to expel breath, the feet were not fastened tightly to the cross; thus the use of the plaque at the head of the nail. With arms outstretched and the legs thrust to one side, the trunk would have been contorted, allowing only one hip to rest on the *sedile*. There, nailed hand and foot, the Son of God chose to die so that the sons and daughters of Adam might find life.

Having carried out their task, the soldiers affixed the *titulus* to the cross and waited for death to come. "When they had finished crucifying him they shared out his clothing by casting lots, and then sat down and stayed there keeping guard over him" (Mt. 27:35-36). The centurion and his retinue had to stay at the execution site to certify that the execution had been carried out and that the man had died. As after the scourging, the Romans have a chance to entertain themselves at the expense of their victim.

Jesus is now introduced to new horrors of Roman "genius." Slowly his head clears from the shock of pain caused by the nails ripping through his limbs. Even with the aid of the *sedile*, his body hangs from the nails which hold his arms outstretched, causing the muscles in the chest to spasm; this downward thrust of the body impedes the movement of the diaphragm, making it impossible to expel the air which has been brought into the lungs. Eventually, the lungs would feel like balloons about to pop. In order to relieve the strain of his upper body, Jesus pushes his body weight up, only to experience a new burst of pain as his weight bears down on the nail through his feet. Not only does he feel the explosion of pain radiating up the legs from where the nail pierced the heel, but as he drives his body upwards, his lacerated back scrapes against the rough surface of the cross. Every aspect of his crucifixion was designed to inflict the maximum amount of pain, while prolonging the agony which would lead to the actual moment of death.

Thirteen

"When I Am Lifted Up"

The Seven Last Words:
The Cup Is Drained to the Last Drop

O Sacred Head Now Wounded

O sacred head, now wounded
    with grief and shame weighed down,
Now scornfully surrounded
    with thorns, thine only crown:
How pale thou art with anguish,
    with sore abuse and scorn
How does that visage languish
    which once was bright as morn!

What thou, my Lord, hast suffered
    was all for sinners, gain;
Mine, mine was the transgression,
    but thine the deadly pain.
Lo, here I fall, my Savior
    'Tis I deserve thy place;
Look on me with thy favor,
    vouchsafe to me thy grace.

What language shall I borrow
    to thank thee, dearest friend,
For this thy dying sorrow,
    thy pity without end?
O make me thine forever;
    and should I fainting be,
Lord, let me never, never
    outlive my love for thee.

"The passers-by jeered at him; they shook their heads and said, 'Aha! So you would destroy the Temple and rebuild it in three days! Then save yourself: come down from the cross!' The chief priests and the scribes mocked him among themselves in the same way. 'He saved others,' they said 'he cannot ·save himself. Let the Christ, the King of Israel, come down from the cross now for us to see it and then we will believe.' Even those who were crucified with him taunted him" (Mk. 15:29-32). The shouts and noise which had deafened the crowd to the Truth now are sounded again. There is no silent breeze in which to hear the Father's voice, only the shouts of hatred and bigotry, only the sounds of the infernal din.

Impaled on the tree, God's champion, our *goel*, confronts the Prince of Darkness. The faithful band of disciples are gone. The adoring angels veil their faces at the sight. Only a few sympathetic women stand at the foot of the cross. They see what no human eye should ever be allowed to see: the innocent body of the Word made Flesh covered with bleeding weals and nailed to the gibbet of the cross.

Despite the fact that movie versions of Good Friday depict crowds of thousands gathering for Jesus' trial, one gets the feeling while reading the gospel accounts that very few people actually followed Jesus to the top of the hill of Calvary. Daniel-Rops offers this sobering reflection.

> A condemned man being led to the place of execution was not very uncommon. And when all was over, when the three crosses, the Cross of Christ and those of the two thieves, stood upon the bare mound of Golgotha, that haunt of wandering dogs and vultures, it is doubtful that many of the travelers on the road stopped to gaze at those poor remnants of humanity, to read an inscription placed on the central cross and to ask the soldiers as they played at knuckle bones, "Who is it?" In the daily life of the Jewish people, may not the most important event in the history of the world have passed unnoticed? *(Daily Life in the Time of Jesus)*

Father Forgive Them

"When they reached the place of the Skull, they crucified him there and the two criminals also, one on the right, the other on the left. Jesus said, 'Father, forgive them; they do not know what they are doing'" (Lk. 23:33-34). Neither the centurion nor his cohort, neither Pilate nor Caiaphas, neither the crowds nor the criminals crucified with Jesus were aware of the real reason for this gruesome sight. Only those who look at the cross and read the third chapter of Genesis can know what really is at stake. Jesus knows the ignorance of the people and offers a plea in their behalf. Jesus prays that their blindness would be healed so that they could be drawn towards the Light. "And when I am lifted up from the earth, I shall draw all men to myself" (Jn. 12:32).

The immediate reaction Jesus got from those who saw his tortured body stretched upon the wood of the cross was neither compassion nor belief.

> The passers-by jeered at him; they shook their heads and said, "So you would destroy the Temple and rebuild it in three days! Then save yourself! If you are God's son, come down from the cross!" The chief priests with the scribes and elders mocked him in the same way. "He saved others;" they said "he cannot save himself. He is the king of Israel; let him come down from the cross now, and we will believe in him. He put his trust in God; now let God rescue him if he wants him. For he did say: 'I am the son of God?'" Even the robbers who were crucified with him taunted him in the same way (Mt. 27:39-44).

The people did not know their day of visitation. They could not see the Holy One of Israel who was in their midst. As he did to the woman at the well, he would say to them if he could, "If you only knew what God is offering and who it is that is saying to you: Give me a drink, you would have been the one to ask, and he would have given you living water" (Jn. 4:10). As it is, he can only pray, "Father, forgive them," as life slowly ebbs from his body. He does not come down from the cross to save his own life; rather, he clings to the nails, knowing that is the only way he will save the human race.

"The Lord Yahweh comes to my help, so that I am untouched by the insults. So, too, I set my face like flint; I know I shall not be shamed" (Is. 50:7). Tradition has helped us to see and understand the life, mission, and passover of Jesus in terms of the Suffering Servant of Isaiah. As Jesus absorbs the pain of the world; as Jesus takes into himself the insults heaped upon him, he becomes the source of peace and healing to those who look to him. In his wounds we see our own woundedness and are healed.

This Day You Will Be With Me in Paradise

"One of the criminals hanging there abused him. 'Are you not the Christ?' he said. 'Save yourself and us as well.' But the other spoke up and rebuked him. 'Have you no fear of God at all?' he said. 'You got the same sentence as he did, but in our case we deserved it: we are paying for what we did. But this man has done nothing wrong. Jesus,' he said 'remember me when you come into your kingdom.' 'Indeed, I promise you,' he replied, 'today you will be with me in paradise'" (Lk. 23:39-43). People who came to Jesus, as well as those who were brought to Jesus, were looking for compassion and healing. He greeted them with words of love and forgiveness, reconciling them with the Father. "Seeing their faith, Jesus said to the paralytic, 'Courage, my child, your sins are forgiven.' And at this some scribes said to themselves, 'This man is blaspheming'" (Mt. 9:2-3). Those who would accuse him of blasphemy would not turn to him for forgiveness. They could not accept the time of visitation. They did not recognize the presence of the Holy One of Israel. Yet, a social outcast who knows himself to be under the curse of death turns to the crucified one and asks for life. There can be no pretense, no excuses. With the truth comes the path to life, and there one finds life without end.

My God, My God, Why Have You Deserted Me?

"We had all gone astray like sheep, each taking his own way, and Yahweh burdened him with the sins of us all" (Is. 53:6). It has been said that the truth of being can only be made known in its opposite; e.g. love is revealed through hatred, unity through fragmentation, and peace through conflict. Standing before the cross, we see the eternal and almighty God revealed in the tortured and crucified Jesus. "From the sixth hour there was darkness over all the land until the ninth hour. And about the ninth hour, Jesus cried out in a loud voice, *'Eli, Eli, lama sabachthani?'* that is, 'My God, my God, why have you deserted me?'" (Mt. 27:45-46). The greatest torment that Jesus had to endure was this feeling of abandonment by God. This feeling of utter nothingness leads us to understand what happened on the cross and something which took place between Jesus and his Father. Jesus remained obedient while he knew the Father's love and presence, but would he remain steadfast if this reassurance were withdrawn? In this cry from the cross, Jesus is putting everything at stake, his human existence and his divine, as well as his entire message concerning the presence of the kingdom of God. Ultimately, in this moment of abandonment and apparent rejection the deity of the One whom he called "Father" is at stake. This cry must certainly have caused the disciples to question the validity of Jesus prayer at the Last Supper: "Father, may they be one in us, as you are in me and I am in you, so that the world may believe it was you who sent me. I have given them the glory you gave me, that they may be one as we are one" (Jn. 17:21-22).

The Book of Job also affords us some insight into this problem of distance experienced by one who is beloved of God.

> In all this Job committed no sin nor offered any insult to God. Once again the Sons of God came to attend on Yahweh, and among them was Satan. So Yahweh said to Satan, "Where have you been?" "Round the earth," he answered "roaming about." So Yahweh asked him, "Did you notice my servant Job? There is no one like him on the earth: a sound and honest man who fears God and shuns evil. His life continues blameless as ever; in vain you provoked me to ruin him" (Jb. 1:22–2:3).

Thus we see the reason for the holding back of God's face, even from his only-begotten Son. The antagonist, Satan, has received permission to put Jesus to the ultimate test: absolute destitution of spirit. Throughout it all, like Job, Jesus feels totally alienated from the One whom he has called "my Father," "my God." "I cry to you, and you give me no answer; I stand before you, but you take no notice. You have grown cruel in your dealing with me, your hand lies on me, heavy and hostile. You carry me up to ride the wind, tossing me about in a tempest. I know it is to death that you are taking me, the common meeting place of all that live" (Jb. 30:20-23). Let no one try to minimize this feeling of desolation as mere depression. Jesus had to unite himself so totally to the human condition that he felt in his very being the curse of sinners, the rejection of people whom God had once called his own. We find a description of this in the prophet Isaiah. "I did forsake you for a brief moment, but with great love will I take you back. In excess of anger, for a moment I hid my face from you. But with everlasting love I have taken pity on you, says Yahweh, your redeemer" (Is. 54:8).

This Is Your Mother

Jesus is the Son of God, our redeemer. He loves us with an everlasting love. Hanging on the cross, he shows his love and tenderness in a very simple way: he offers us the love of the woman who gave him life. "Near the cross of Jesus stood his mother and his mother's sister, Mary the wife of Clopas, and Mary of Magdala. Seeing his mother and the disciple he loved standing near her, Jesus said to his mother, 'Woman, this is your son.' Then to the disciple he said, 'This is your mother.' And from that moment the disciple made a place for her in his home" (Jn. 19:25-27). Standing at the foot of the cross, the woman looks up at the fruit of her womb, crucified for us. Like the first Eve, she sees that this fruit is desirable. The voice from the tree tells her not to grasp this fruit but to turn and embrace the child standing at her side. Similarly, the beloved disciple must learn to cling to the woman whom Jesus has entrusted to his care and find room for her and all her children in his house. He must make his world large enough to include others and these he will have to serve, as his Master had taught.

"His mother and brothers now arrived and, standing out-side, sent in a message asking for him. A crowd was sitting around him at the time the message was passed to him, 'Your mother and brothers and sisters are outside asking for you.' He replied, 'Who are my mother and my brothers?' And looking round at those sitting in a circle about him, he said, 'Here are my mother and my brothers. Anyone who does the will of God, that person is my brother and sister and mother'" (Mk. 3:31-35). The path that leads us into the kingdom is found in obedience to God's will. While hanging on the cross, Jesus gave us his mother to be our mother and guide. Mary knew herself to be the "handmaid of the Lord" and she tells us to do whatever her son commands us. Like John, we are to cherish this woman and find a special place for her in our daily lives.

St. John Chrysostom gave expression to this filial devotion and imitation in his hymn to the Mother of God.

> It is truly proper to glorify you, who have borne God,
> the Ever-blessed, Immaculate, and the Mother of our God.
> More honorable than the Cherubim,
> and beyond compare more glorious than the Seraphim,
> who, a virgin, gave birth to God the Word,
> you, truly the Mother of God, we magnify.

I Am Thirsty

"After this, Jesus knew that everything had now been completed, and to fulfill the Scriptures perfectly he said: 'I am thirsty'" (Jn. 19:28). We know of the pain and suffering of flogging and crucifixion. Rarely do we stop to think of the tremendous fever which must have burned in Jesus' body as a result of the torture he endured. Given the loss of blood, compounded with the loss of body fluid through the pores, the thirst produced by this state of dehydration must have been extreme. "I am like water draining away, my bones are all disjointed, my heart is like wax, melting inside me; my palate is drier than a potsherd and my tongue is stuck to my jaw" (Ps. 22:14-15).

One finds a moving reflection on the thirst or dryness of Jesus in the writings of Julian of Norwich.

> I saw four ways in which the body dried. The first was
> through bloodlessness, the second was the consequent
> of pain, the third was that he was hanging up in the air
> as people hang up a cloth to dry, the fourth was that his

physical nature needed liquid, and there was no kind of comfort ministered to him. Ah, hard and grievous was the pain, but it was far harder and more grievous when the fluid failed and everything began to dry, shrivelling so *(Showings)*.

The thirst of Jesus reveals the depths of his agony. No angels came to minister to him, neither was there any word from the Father. Nailed to the cross, Jesus found himself plunged into the deepest and darkest of black holes. The darkness that he experienced seemed to engulf the whole cosmos. "When the sixth hour came there was darkness over the whole land until the ninth hour" (Mk. 15:33). Through it all, however, Jesus remains the faithful servant, obedient to his Father's, will. There, as the darkness thickens, Jesus grasps hold of his infernal foe, preparing to claim the victory. This moment is written of in the prologue of John's gospel. "In the beginning was the Word: the Word was with God and the Word was God. He was with God in the beginning. Through him all things came to be, not one thing had its being but through him. All that came to be had life in him and that life was the light of men, a light that shines in the dark, a light that darkness could not overpower" (Jn. 1:1-5).

It Is Accomplished

The pain, agony and suffering of Christ's passion touched every fiber of his being, body, soul and spirit. "Like a sapling he grew up in front of us, like a root in arid ground. Without beauty, without majesty we saw him, no looks to attract our eyes; a thing despised and rejected by men, a man of sorrows and familiar with suffering, a man to make people screen their faces; he was despised and we took no account of him" (Is. 53:2-3). In him was left neither strength nor vigor. Physical weakness would cause him to hang at length from the nails in his wrists, the spasms in his chest would overwhelm him, causing him to thrust upward upon the nail through his heels, sending new shocks of pain through his body. Julian of Norwich offers this thought:

But our true Mother Jesus, he alone bears us for joy and for endless life, blessed may he be. So he carries us within him in love and travail, until the full time which he wanted to suffer the sharpest thorns and cruel pains that ever were or will be, and at the last he died. And when he had finished, and had borne us so for bliss, still all this could not satisfy his wonderful love. And he revealed this in these great surpassing words of love: If I could suffer more, I would suffer more. He could not die any more, but he did not want to cease working; therefore he must needs nourish us, for the precious love of motherhood has made him our debtor (*Showings*).

Jesus had taken the cup which would not pass away. He had drained it and left no painful drought for anyone else to sample. Because he loved us, we who are his disciples are free from the chains of death. "Awake, awake! To your feet, Jerusalem! You who from Yahweh's hand have drunk the cup of his wrath. The cup of stupor you have drained to the dregs" (Is. 51:17). In his thirst, Jesus gulps down the cup of suffering and pain, the cup of judgment and condemnation. In his emptiness, we find fullness. "A jar of vinegar stood there, so putting a sponge soaked in the vinegar on a hyssop stick they held it up to his mouth. After Jesus had taken the vinegar he said, 'It is accomplished'" (Jn. 19:29-30).

Father, Into Your Hands I Commit My Spirit

Jesus, being Son of God and Son of Man, drank the cup of wrath and retribution which was rightfully ours to drink. In so doing, he destroyed the veil which once separated us from God. "The veil of the Temple was torn right down the middle" (Lk. 23:45). In the love of Christ and in his obedience to the Father, God and man are reconciled because sin and death are conquered. The all-consuming love of the Father consumes the Son as an acceptable oblation. The pain of his body is nothing compared to the desire of his heart to release the burning fire of love on all created reality. "Oh, that you would tear the heavens open and come down—at your Presence the mountains would melt, as fire sets brushwood alight, as fire causes water to boil—to make known your name to your enemies, and make the nations tremble at your Presence, working unexpected miracles such as no one has ever heard of before" (Is. 64:1-4). God, who chose to become a human being, took to himself all our weakness. Now, impaled on the cross, he embraces all our pain and suffering, thus enabling us to see ourselves for what we really are. Lifted up before our gaze, he draws all the members of the human family to the Father. It is in him that we live and move and have our being. In him: in those limbs nailed fast to the wood of the cross, we find the mystery of God's loving kindness and merciful justice.

Jesus had known rejection in the face of the world. He was deserted by his closest friends. He was condemned by his own people. He was mocked, tortured, and put to death by men much like himself. While he was in his death agony, he felt abandoned by his Father. At no time did he ever turn back from his one objective, to do the Father's will. This obedience was to claim his last breath. "Jesus cried out in a loud voice. He said, 'Father, into your hands I commit my spirit.' With these words he breathed his last" (Lk. 23:46).

O Love Divine, What Hast Thou Done

by Charles Wesley

O Love divine, what hast thou done! The immortal
God hath died for me! The Father's coeternal
Son bore all my sins upon the tree. The immortal
God for me hath died: My Lord, my Love, is crucified!

Is crucified for me and you, to bring us
rebels back to God. Believe, believe the record
true, ye all are bought with Jesus' blood. Pardon for
all flows from his side: My Lord, my Love, is crucified!

Behold him, all ye that pass by, the bleeding
Prince of life and peace! Come, sinners, see your Savior
die, and say, "Was ever grief like his?" Come, feel with
me his blood applied: My Lord, my Love, is crucified!

Fourteen

The Descent into Hades

The Lord of the Living Enters the Abode of the Dead—Death, Where Is Your Sting?

Behold the Savior of Mankind
by Samuel Wesley

Behold the Savior of mankind
nailed to the shameful tree;
how vast the love that him inclined
to bleed and die for thee!

Hark how he groans! while nature shakes,
and earth's strong pillars bend!
The temple's veil in sunder breaks,
the solid marbles rend.

Tis done! the precious ransom's paid!
"Receive my soul!" he cries;
see where he bows his sacred head!
He bows his head and dies!

But soon he'll break death's envious chain
and in full glory shine.
O Lamb of God, was ever pain,
was ever love like thine?

Like two weary fighters who have gone the distance, the combatants lock in one last effort. Both have been drained in the course of the contest, the man raising his heel and the serpent baring his fangs. The heel has felt the pain of the venomous bite; the skull has been ground to the dust. A loud cry rings out, Jesus' body jerks, and then all is silent. The crowd no longer screams for a spectacle, nor does it jeer at the tortured victim. A hush comes over Calvary's hill. "And when all the people who had gathered for the spectacle saw what had happened, they went home beating their breasts" (Lk. 23:48).

When people consider the message and teachings of any charismatic leader, they want to see it authenticated in the way he or she faces death. An example of this is provided for us in Louis Fischer's account of the death of Gandhi.

> At 5:05, Gandhi, troubled because he was late, left Patel and, leaning his arms on Abha and Manu, hurried to the prayer ground. Nathuran Godse had moved into the front row, his hand on the pistol in his pocket. He had no personal hatred of Gandhi, Godse stated at his trial at which he was sentenced to be hanged: "Before I fired the shots I actually wished him well and bowed to him in reverence."

> In response to Godse's obeisance and the reverential bows of other members of the congregation, Gandhi touches his palms together, smiled and blessed them. Manu tried to brush him aside so Gandhi could start services without further delay, Godse pushed her away, planted himself in front of the Mahatma, drew his pistol, pulled the trigger and fired three times. The smile faded from Gandhi's face and his arms fell to his sides. He fell and died murmuring, "Oh, God."

> His legacy is courage, his lesson truth, his weapon love. His life is his monument. He now belongs to mankind (*Gandhi: His Life and Message for the World*).

On that mound, just outside the walls of Jerusalem, the Son of God was nailed to the cross. It was there that he suffered and died that we might have eternal life. Through the cross, God consecrated and sanctified wood, nails, absurdity, and helplessness, making them sacraments of his loving kindness. No doubt the Romans had executed many people, depriving them of all human dignity, tearing strength and vigor from their bodies under the lash, and watching them struggle to breathe as life ebbed from every limb. Thirst brought pleas for drink, while shocks of pains caused by efforts to breathe brought curses upon those who had set the nails. Jesus, however, does not beg for mercy, but offers it, forgiving those who crucified him. Knowing that he is fulfilling the Father's will, which is his whole purpose in life, he surrenders his spirit into the Father's hands. He embodies total resignation and humble submission. "The centurion, who was standing in front of him, had seen how he had died, and he said, 'In truth, this man was a son of God'" (Mk. 15:39).

The remains found in the tomb near Mount Scopus, mentioned in chapter twelve, verify the events which took place after the death of Jesus. Recall that the right tibia of the young man was broken. This fracture was clearly produced by a single, sharp blow. With the heels of both feet being pinned together, the victim's legs would be thrust to one side, in this case towards the left. The left calf would lay across the edge of the cross's upright, with the right calf resting against the left. When the blow was administered to the right leg, the percussion would drive the left against the wood of the cross. The bones of the left calf were broken in a straight sharp-toothed line along the edge of the cross, while the right had large, sharp slivers. Forensic studies would suggest that these fractures were the result of pressure on both sides of the bones: the bludgeoning of the right leg and the resistance of the edge of the cross.

The ossuary found at Mount Scopus provided archaeological information about the Palestinian variation of Roman crucifixion, at least whenever the victim was a Jew. Normally, the Romans would leave the criminal on the cross, allowing for a protracted and agonizing death. The impaled corpses would then serve as ghoulish reminders to the passers-by of Roman justice. However, Jewish religious tradition required that the body be buried on the day of execution. Thus, rather than needlessly offend the people, the Romans modified the process. To insure a hasty death, the victim's legs were broken, making it impossible for him to push himself to an upright position and breathe. The process would be completed so as to allow for burial by nightfall.

The day of Jesus' crucifixion brought added problems: not only was this the eve of the Sabbath but also the beginning of the observance of the high holy days.

It was Preparation Day, and to prevent the bodies' remaining on the cross during the Sabbath—since that Sabbath was a day of special solemnity—the Jews asked Pilate to have the legs broken and the bodies taken away. Consequently the soldiers came and broke the legs of the first man who had been crucified with him and then of the other. When they came to Jesus, they found he was already dead, and so instead of breaking his legs one of the soldiers pierced his side with a lance; and immediately there came out blood and water (Jn. 19:31-34).

The Gospel of John describes the piercing of Jesus' side after his death. The author is quick to emphasize the sudden flow of blood and water which came forth from the wound. Evidence in the passion narratives shows that Jesus had died before the lance pierced his side. Had Jesus shown any sign of life, his legs would have been broken as were those of the two criminals. Forensic medicine suggests that internal injuries caused by the flogging may have been the cause of death. A blood clot may have formed and during one of the strained efforts to breathe, traveled to the heart, thus explaining the loud cry at the moment of death.

The lance was plunged into Jesus' heart to certify his death. John used the Greek word *pleura* which is translated "side" but it also can be taken to mean the ribs or chest cavity. The point of the spear would have passed between the ribs, perforating the lung, and lodged in the heart. As it was withdrawn, the fluids collected around the lungs and the blood from the chamber of the heart would flow from the wound.

The Savior beckons us to his open heart, where we will find drink to satisfy our thirst. From his open side, the church is fashioned and washed clean in the blood of salvation. When we understand this, we, too, will sing the words of this hymn:

The Old Rugged Cross

On a hill far away stood an old rugged cross,
the emblem of suffering and shame;
and I love that old cross where the dearest and best
for a world of lost sinners was slain.

Oh that old rugged cross, so despised by the world,
has a wondrous attraction for me;
for the dear Lamb of God left his glory above
to bear it to dark Calvary.

In that old rugged cross, stained with blood so divine,
O wondrous beauty I see,
for 'twas on that old cross Jesus suffered and died,
to pardon and sanctify me.

To the old rugged cross I will ever be true,
its shame and reproach gladly bear;
thus he'll call me some day to my home far away,
where his glory forever I'll share.
Refrain:
So I'll cherish the old rugged cross,
till my trophies at last I lay down;
I will cling to the old rugged cross,
and exchange it some day for a crown.

Finally, Jesus has given up his life; now burial preparations must be made. "There came a rich man of Arimathea, called Joseph, who had himself become a disciple of Jesus. This man went to Pilate and asked for the body of Jesus" (Mt. 27:57-58). Reading this verse, one is alerted to the fact that Jesus did not limit his outreach to the poor or marginalized people of his day. Anyone who was willing to listen to his words was welcome. To those who received his word, he also entrusted his body. This word takes on sacramental importance as the vocabulary of faith develops. "Pilate, astonished that he should have died so soon, summoned the centurion and inquired if he was already dead. Having been assured of this by the centurion, he granted the corpse to Joseph" (Mk. 15:44-45). The report of the lance thrust would have served as needed proof of the death. The soldiers would then remove the body from the cross and hand it over to the family.

Once the execution was over, the curiosity seekers would go home, leaving friends and relatives to their grief. Burial preparations were completed privately and lovingly. "Joseph took the body, wrapped it in a clean shroud and put it in his own new tomb which he had hewn out of rock" (Mt. 27:59-60). Archaeological finds allow us to imagine the design of the tomb in which Jesus was buried. Tombs were cave-like rooms cut into the soft limestone which abounds in the region. Outside the entrance would be found a forecourt. Inside the entrance was a large chamber; along three sides of this chamber were stone benches. These benches could be used as work tables upon which the body was cleaned, anointed and wrapped in the shroud. Once prepared, the body would be placed in a burial niche.

"They took the body of Jesus and wrapped it with the spices in linen clothes, following the Jewish burial custom" (Jn. 19:40). As the disciples paid their last tribute of service to the Master, they may have recalled his preaching about the grain of wheat: "I tell you most solemnly, unless a wheat grain falls on the ground and dies, it remains only a single grain; but if it dies, it yields a rich harvest" (Jn. 12:23-24).

Let us suppose the tomb in which Jesus was buried had an outer court. From such an atrium, the women could have observed the burial preparations. "Now Mary of Magdala and the other Mary were there, sitting opposite the sepulchre" (Mt. 27:61). With Mary and the other witnesses we stand outside the tomb and sing hymns of praise to the Father.

> O joyful Light! Light and Holy Glory of the Father immortal, the heavenly, holy, the Blessed One, O Jesus Christ. Now that we have reached the setting of the sun, and see the evening light, we sing to God, Father, Son and Holy Spirit. It is fitting at all times to raise a song of praise in measured melody to you, O Son of God, the giver of life. Behold the universe sings your glory" (Hymn of the Evening from the Byzantine Vespers).

The notes drift off in the wind, and the labor of love is soon finished; the disciples emerge from the burial vault.

"He then rolled a stone against the entrance to the tomb" (Mk. 15:46). The entrance to the tomb was rather small, perhaps allowing access to one person at a time. Most of the tombs which have been discovered were sealed with the use of a rolling stone, a stone disc which was set on its edge. The stone would be fitted into a track and often could be moved by one person. The closure was never meant to be permanent because of the need to reuse a burial place. This may seem strange to us, but unlike the American practice, graves were reused. In that embalming was not done, the bodies were not preserved from decomposition. The burial niche was only a temporary resting place in which the body was allowed to decompose. About a year after burial, a member of the family would return to the tomb and gather up the dried bones. These would be placed in an ossuary (if they were people of means) or placed in a common grave. There is reason to believe this practice of carefully gathering up the bones after the flesh had decayed had religious significance most especially connected with the notion of resurrection. "Jesus said to Martha 'Your brother will rise again.' Martha said, 'I know he will rise again at the resurrection on the last day.' Jesus said, 'I am the resurrection. If anyone believe in me, even though he dies he will live, and whoever lives and believes in me will never die'" (Jn. 11:23-26).

It is not unreasonable to assume that the disciples gathered outside the tomb for a memorial prayer before returning to their homes for the Sabbath. "Hear, O Israel, the Lord our God, the Lord is One. Blessed are you, O God of the Universe. Bless your servant with peace. Let his memory live on in the hearts of all those who loved him. May the beauty of his life abide among us as a blessing. Amen" (taken from the *New Union Prayer Book*).

The Byzantine Liturgy has an interesting prayer which captures the paradox of Jesus' burial. "When your body was in the tomb, and your soul in Hades, when you were in paradise with the thief, You were at the same time, O Christ, as God upon your throne with the Father and the Spirit—infinite and filling all things" *(Prayer at the end of the Preparation of the Gifts)*. When the Immortal God entered into the Land of Hades, all that was mortal was set free. Jesus' death on the cross won him entry into Satan's domain, where he set the souls of the just free. The tradition of Jesus' descent into Hades finds its earliest expression in the First Letter of St. Peter. "Why, Christ himself, innocent though he was, had died once for sins, died for the guilty, to lead us to God. In the body he was put to death, in the spirit he was raised to life, and in the spirit, he went to preach to the spirits in prison—Hades" (1 Pt. 3:18-19). Satan was defeated, the head of the serpent had been crushed. Now, while his body lay in the recesses of the tomb, Jesus took possession of his spoils. The gates of Sheol were broken; the bonds of death were torn asunder. The Light of Life shone upon the souls held in the shadow of death. The Lord of Life embraces Adam and Eve and leads them into eternal light.

> Today a great silence reigns on earth, a great silence and a great stillness. A great silence because the King is asleep. The earth trembled and is still because God has fallen asleep in the flesh and he has raised up all who have slept ever since the world began. . . . He has gone in search of Adam, our first father, as for a lost sheep. Greatly desiring to visit those who live in darkness and the shadow of death, he has gone to free from sorrow Adam in his bonds and Eve, captive with him—He who is both their God and the son of Eve. . . . "I am your God, who for your sake have become your son. . . . I order you, O sleeper, to awake. I did not create you to be a prisoner in hell. Rise from the dead, for I am the life of the dead" *(Catechism of the Catholic Church, #635)*.

"When you descended to death, O Immortal Life, you destroyed the Abyss by the radiance of your divinity. And when you raised the dead from the depths of the earth all the heavenly powers cried out: O Giver of Life, Christ our God, glory be to you" *(Tropar for Easter Matins)*.

Fifteen
The Third Day
Christ Is Risen! Indeed, He Is Risen!

Third Antiphon for Easter (Byzantine Rite)

Refrain:

Christ is risen from the dead!
By death he conquered death,
and to those in the graves he granted life.

Let God arise and let his enemies be scattered,
and let those who hate him flee before his face.

As smoke vanishes, so let them vanish,
as wax melts before a fire.

So let the wicked perish at the presence of God,
and let the righteous ones rejoice.

This is the day that the Lord has made;
let us exult and rejoice in it.

The Sabbath rest over, the Lord of Life comes forth from his chamber. Creation experiences a new beginning. "And all at once there was a violent earthquake, for the angel of the Lord, descending from heaven came and rolled away the stone and sat on it" (Mt. 28:2). The God of Life now leaves the territory of Sheol, the underworld, and returns to the earth which he has created. All of creation shudders at the nearness of its God. "The sea fled at the sight, the Jordan stopped flowing, the mountains skipped like rams, and like lambs, the hills" (Ps. 114:3-4). Christ has conquered death by enduring it. Now neither death nor the grave have any power over the Son of God. He who had hung helpless on the cross, who had suffered death and endured the confinement of the tomb, now comes forth from the grave full of power and might, clothed in glory and light, never to die again.

The scriptures tell us that the women came to the tomb carrying spices. "When the Sabbath was over, Mary of Magdala, Mary the mother of James, and Salome, bought spices with which to go and anoint him. And very early in the morning on the first day of the week they went to the tomb, just as the sun was rising" (Mk. 16:1-2). If nearly one hundred pounds of spice were used when Jesus' body was placed in the tomb, why would they be carrying more now? If the burial preparations were completed on Friday, why were the women bringing more ointments to the tomb? Had Mary of Magdala become so identified with the way she anointed Jesus' feet that she is depicted as "the ointment bearer"? Possibly, the women were preparing to return to their homes and wanted to make one last visit to the final resting place of their Master. Having walked with him and heard his preaching, they would now have to return to their former way of life. Could they ever really go back? The artistry of the text shows these pilgrims coming into the garden just as the darkness of the old day was giving way to the dawning of the new day.

The readers of the gospels were not Jews, for the most part. It is possible that they had heard of the use of spices at the end of the Sabbath and added its use to the resurrection story. Jewish Sabbath observance ends with a ritual of smelling a box of spices. As he holds the spice box, the head of the house says,

> The added soul the Sabbath confers is leaving now, and these spices will console us at the moment of its passing. They remind us that the six days will pass, and Sabbath will return. And their bouquet will make us yearn with thankful heart for the sweetness of rest, and the fragrance of growing things; for the clean smell of rainwashed earth and the sad innocence of childhood, and for the dream of a world healed of pain, pure and wholesome as on that first Sabbath, when God, finding his handiwork good rested from the work of creation *(New Union Prayer Book)*.

It is this remembering of happier times and waiting with anticipation that brings the women to the tomb. Simone Weil once said, "Waiting patiently in expectation is the foundation of the spiritual life."

We turn again to the *New Union Prayer Book* for a beautiful reflection on the kindling of the first fire of the new week. The imagery contained in these passages is very similar to that of the women coming to the tomb just as the New Day began.

> The Rabbis tell us: As night descended at the end of the world's first Sabbath, Adam feared and wept. Then God showed him how to make a fire, and by its light and warmth to dispel the darkness and its terrors. Kindling flame is a symbol of our first labor upon the earth.
>
> Sabbath departs and the workday begins as we kindle fire. And we, who dread the night no more, thank God for the flame by which we turn earth's raw stuff into things of use and beauty.
>
> The Havdalah candle's double wick reminds us that all qualities are paired. We have the power to create many different fires, some useful, others baneful. Let us be on guard never to let this gift of fire devour human life, sear cities and scorch fields, or foul the pure air of heaven, obscuring the very skies. Let the fire we kindle be holy; let it bring light and warmth to all humanity.
>
> Blessed is the Lord our God, Ruler of the Universe, who separates sacred from profane, light from darkness, the seventh day of rest from the six days of labor.

The Lord our God, the Creator of the Universe, who gave Adam and Eve fire to dispel the darkness of night, has sent his Son, the Light of Life, into Hades, the region of darkness and death, to bring Adam and Eve to the kingdom of Light. With the setting of the sun, the Sabbath departs, and Jesus rises from the dead to provide the world with a new Light which casts out all darkness. This passage from the darkness of night to the glory of the resurrection is expressed in the closing verses of the Easter Proclamation.

> Therefore, heavenly Father, in the joy of this night, receive our evening sacrifice of praise, your Church's solemn offering. Accept this Easter candle, a flame divided but undimmed, a pillar of fire that flows to the honor of God. Let it mingle with the lights of heaven and continue bravely burning to dispel the darkness of this night. May the Morning Star which never sets find this flame still burning: Christ, that Morning Star, who came back from the dead, and shed his peaceful light on all mankind, Your Son who lives and reigns for ever and ever *(Exultet)*.

Jesus' resurrection is the keystone of our Christian faith. From its very beginning, the church has taught this irreducible tenet: on the third day Jesus rose from the dead. The earliest records of apostolic preaching make it clear that the bodily resurrection of the crucified Lord was the validation of all that he said and did.

> Men of Israel, listen to what I am going to say: Jesus the Nazarene was a man commended to you by God by the miracles and portents and signs that God worked through him when he was among you, as you all know. This man, who was put into your power by the deliberate intention and foreknowledge of God, you took and had crucified by men outside the Law. You killed him, but God raised him to life, freeing him from the pangs of Hades (Acts 2:22-23).

The resurrection of Jesus from the dead is the foundation upon which all the rest of our belief rests.

St. Paul is quite emphatic about this:

> Now if Christ raised from the dead is what has been preached, how can some of you be saying that there is no resurrection of the dead? If there is no resurrection of the dead, Christ himself cannot have been raised, and if Christ has not been raised then our preaching is useless and your believing it is useless; indeed, we are shown up as witnesses who have committed perjury

before God, because we swore in evidence before God
that he had raised Christ to life. For if the dead are not
raised, Christ has not been raised, and if Christ has not
been raised, you are still in your sins. And what is more
serious, all who have died in Christ have perished. If
our hope in Christ has been for this life only, we are the
most unfortunate of all people (1 Cor. 15:12-19).

Despite the fact that the resurrection of Jesus from the dead
is the central doctrine of Christian belief, it is also one of the
most problematic. No one actually saw Jesus rise. No one witnessed his leaving the tomb. The gospel narratives give con-
flicting accounts. Although some of the specific details do not
agree, the central and most basic element of the earliest gospel
tradition is that the tomb was empty when the women came to
it. "Some women from our group have astounded us: they
went to the tomb in the early morning, and when they did not
find the body, they came back to tell us they had seen a vision
of angels who declared he was alive" (Lk. 24:22-23). The empty
tomb was the first evidence of the resurrection; the apparition
stories come later.

To make sure that the reader does not miss the significance
of this discovery, the evangelist adds the announcement of the
angel. "On entering the tomb the women saw a young man in
a white robe on the right-hand side, and they were struck with
amazement. But he said to them, 'There is no need for alarm.
You are looking for Jesus of Nazareth, who was crucified: he
has risen, he is not here. See, here is the place where they laid
him'" (Mk.16:5-6). The tomb is empty because the Lord of Life
has conquered death and death has no hold on him. This
theme is taken up by many of the early Fathers of the Church.

> Let no one grieve over his poverty, for the universal
> kingdom has been revealed; let no one weep over his
> sins, for pardon has shone from the grave; let no one
> fear death, for the death of our Savior has set us free: he
> has destroyed it by enduring it, he has despoiled Hades
> by going down into its kingdom, he has angered it by
> allowing it to taste of his flesh. When Isaiah foresaw all
> this he cried out: "O Hades, you have been angered by

encountering him in the nether world." Hades is angered because it is frustrated, it is angered because it has been mocked, it is angered because it has been destroyed, it is angered because it has been reduced to nothing, it is angered because it is now captive. It seized a body, and, behold, it discovered God. It seized earth, and, behold, it encountered heaven. It seized the visible, and was overcome by the invisible.

"O death, where is your sting? O Hades, where is your victory?" Christ is risen and you are abolished, Christ is risen and the demons are cast down, Christ is risen and the angels rejoice, Christ is risen and life is freed, Christ is risen and the tomb is emptied of the dead: for Christ, being risen from the dead, has become the Leader and Reviver of those who had fallen asleep. To him be glory and power for ever and ever. Amen. (Resurrection Homily of St. John Chrysostom)

In addition to the accounts of the discovery of the empty tomb by the women, the New Testament records various post-resurrection appearances of Jesus.

Well then, in the first place, I taught you what I have been taught myself, namely that Christ died for our sins, in accordance with the Scriptures; that he was buried; and that he was raised to life on the third day, in accordance with the Scriptures; that he appeared first to Cephas and secondly to the Twelve. Next he appeared to more than five hundred of the brothers at the same time, most of whom are still alive, though some have died; then he appeared to James and then to all the apostles; and last of all he appeared to me too; it was as though I was born when no one expected it (1 Cor. 15:3-8).

Interestingly, Paul does not mention the appearance to Mary of Magdala, although she is listed first in all the gospel accounts. "Having risen in the morning on the first day of the week, he appeared first to Mary of Magdala from whom he had cast out seven devils. She then went to those who had been his companions, and who were mourning and in tears, and told them. But they did not believe her when they heard her say that he was alive and that she had seen him" (Mk. 16:9-11).

Mary goes to the garden overwhelmed with grief. The Master whom she respected, for whom she had a great affection, had been tortured and put to death. She was the last to leave the tomb, carefully watching the burial preparations. She watched as the stone was rolled into place, securing the entrance to the vault where the body lay. The comfort she had felt, knowing that the Lord's body had been properly laid in the tomb is quickly shattered when she finds the stone rolled away and the body missing. First, the one she loves is taken from her, and now, his body is stolen. Not knowing where to go, she sits outside the tomb sobbing, shedding anxious tears, longing to see the one she loves.

In the Garden

I come to the garden alone, while the dew is still on the roses;

And the voice I hear falling on my ear, the Son of God discloses.

He speaks, and the sound of his voice is so sweet the birds hush their singing;

And the melody that He gave to me within my heart is ringing.

I'd stay in the garden with Him tho' the night around me be falling;

But He bids me go through the voice of woe, His voice to me is calling.

Refrain:

And he walks with me, and he talks with me, and he tells me I am his own,

And the joy we share as we tarry there, none other has ever known.

Mary said, "They have taken my Lord away and I don't know where they have put him." As she said this she turned round and saw Jesus standing there, though she did not recognize him. Jesus said, "Woman, why are you weeping? Who are you looking for?" Supposing him to be the gardener, she said, "Sir, if you have taken him away, tell me where you have put him, and I will go and remove him." Jesus said, "Mary!" She knew him then and said to him in Hebrew, "Rabbuni!"— which means Master (Jn. 20:13-16).

It is significant that Mary recognizes the Lord the moment he calls her by name. With that loving utterance he tears away the veil from her eyes. "The nations then will see your integrity, all the kings give glory, and you will be called by a new name, one which the mouth of Yahweh will confer" (Is. 62:2). The Lord knows us intimately and individually—by name. "If anyone has ears to hear, let him listen to what the Spirit is saying to the churches: to those who prove victorious will give the hidden manna and a white stone—a stone with a name written on it, known only to the one who receives it" (Rv. 2:17).

Mary was drawn out of the depths of her sorrow and pain when the Lord called her name. On another morning, Jesus will speak to "Simon, son of John" and release him from his guilt and shame. The Risen One calls to each of us who have been baptized and invites us to be partakers of the fullness of life. That familiar voice echoes in our hearts, and we are filled with joy. We may not know the exact details of Easter Sunday, but we do know that something extraordinary happened in Jerusalem after Good Friday. The events of Easter Sunday gave new courage and hope to the disciples who a few days earlier ran and hid, fearing for their lives. Hearing the Lord call their names, they throw open the doors and proclaim the good news of the resurrection.

The Paschal Mystery is Christ at the summit of the revelation of the inscrutable mystery of God. It is precisely then that the words pronounced in the Upper Room are completely fulfilled: "He who has seen me has seen the Father." In fact, Christ, whom the Father "did not spare" for our sake and who in his Passion and in the torment of the Cross did not obtain human mercy, has revealed in his resurrection the fullness of the love that the Father has for him and, in him, for all people. "He is not the God of the dead, but of the living." In his Resurrection, Christ has revealed the God of merciful love, precisely because he accepted the Cross as the way to the Resurrection *(Rich in Mercy, by John Paul II)*.

References

A Grief Observed. C. S. Lewis. The Seabury Press, New York, 1961.

A Testament of Hope: The Essential Writings and Speeches of Martin Luther King, Jr. Edited by James M. Washington. Harper Collins, New York, 1991.

Catechism of the Catholic Church. Liguori Publications, Liguori, MO, 1994.

"Crucifixion: Archaeological Evidence." Vassilio Tzafiris. *Biblical Archaeological Review,* Vol. XI, No. 1 (Jan/Feb, 1985), pp. 44ff.

Daily Life in the Time of Jesus. Henri Daniel-Rops. Hawthorne Books, New York, 1962.

Gandhi: His Life and Message for the World. Louis Fischer. Mentor Books, New York, 1964.

Gates of Prayer—The New Union Prayerbook. Central Conference of American Rabbis, New York, 1975.

Liturgy of Holy Week of the Byzantine Rite. Byzantine Seminary Press, Pittsburgh, 1980.

Murder in the Cathedral. T. S. Eliot. Harcourt Brace, New York, 1964.

"Nonviolence and Racial Justice." Martin Luther King, Jr. *Christian Century,* Vol. 74 (February 6, 1957), pp. 165-167.

Peter the Great. Robert K. Massie. Victor Gollancz Ltd., London, 1981.

Rich in Mercy. John Paul II. St. Paul Editions, Boston, 1994.

Seven Pillars of Wisdom. T. E. Lawrence. Dell Publishing Co. Inc., New York, 1993.

Showings. Julian of Norwich. Paulist Press, New York, 1978.

The Divine Liturgy of Our Father St. John Chrysostom. Byzantine Seminary Press, Pittsburgh, 1976.

The Forty Days of Musa Dagh. Franz Werfel. The Viking Press, New York, 1934.

The Passover Haggadah. Schocken Books, New York, 1969.

The Rule of St. Benedict in English. The Liturgical Press, Collegeville, MN, 1982.

The Sacramentary. Catholic Book Publishing Co., New York, 1974.

The Screwtape Letters. C. S. Lewis. Macmillan Co., New York, 1958.

The United Methodist Hymnal. The United Methodist Publishing House, Nashville, TN, 1989.

Till We Have Faces. C. S. Lewis. Wm. B. Eerdmans Publishing Co., Grand Rapids, MI, 1966.